This book is dedicated to the memory of my father and mother, Charles Vernon and Marjorie Beryl Dalton who did much to encourage my love of wild life and the countryside.

Acknowledgments

Illustrations by C.F. Tunnicliffe OBE RA © Estate of C.F.Tunnicliffe.

Cover picture and frontispiece by Philip Snow BA.

The author also acknowledges the kind assistance of Ken Broughton, Secretary of the Charles Tunnicliffe Society, in researching and locating images from the society's records.

WATER UNDER THE BRIDGE

Encounters with nature and extracts from a country diary.

◆

Francis Dalton

CONTENTS

CHAPTER I

A Rural Awakening

We can all recall, I think, at least one significant event or experience which proved to be a turning point in our lives, and for me, this happened when I bought a farm.

It was 1976, at the start of that long hot summer when a new chapter in my life began. The farm, and in particular the farm house which is listed and dates back in part some two hundred and fifty years occupies a quiet corner of rural Nottinghamshire, at the meeting point of three parish boundaries and surrounded by open countryside.

I remember the date, 20th May, because it was sold by auction and took a hefty mortgage and all but my last few pounds to complete the purchase. In truth I spent my life savings and more on what seems in retrospect to have been a major gamble.

Just what the future had in store I had no way of knowing, but I must confess I felt more than a tinge of excitement at the possibility of returning to the countryside I knew and loved as a child.

Life within the Nottingham city boundaries during much of my adult life up to this point had its advantages but I was always a 'country boy' at heart and the memories of my early years growing up in a village never left me and seemed now to be enticing me back.

The daily milk delivery ladled direct from the churn by our neighbouring farmer, finding a barn owl's nest in a roadside hollow tree when walking home from the railway station, the colourful maypole at the village school and my first harvest festival with its display of flowers, fruit and vegetables in the little priory church, all stay with me to this day.

I clearly recall the severe winter of 1947, and the deep snow which lay for weeks, the mixture of curiosity and apprehension when the horse drawn gypsy caravans came by from time to time, and the lingering smell of tar and the sight and sound of the steam roller when the road menders were about.

All these images, and more, from my childhood left a lasting impression and are part of who I am somehow.

Country living has changed much since those days, but to my delight and some surprise I was to discover again the close contact with the natural world which had meant so much during my formative years. Even so, it was with some trepidation that I stepped back from my comfortable life in the suburbs and made the decision to go and view a farmhouse, which remarkably and entirely by coincidence, was situated within a mile of the house in which I was born.

Interestingly, although I was raised nearby I had never laid eyes on the property before, nor even knew of its existence. The farm was hidden away about a quarter of a mile from the road and approached by means of a stony track, full of pot holes and frequented at the time of my first visit by migrant wheatears, their white rumps flashing as they bobbed up and down and flitted between the fence posts.

It was early spring and for me a journey in to the unknown. I was unsure what to expect, but as the car rounded the bend in the track I caught my breath. This was my first glimpse of the farm, and yet something tangible and deep within me seemed instantly to say that this could be my destiny, if only I could make it happen.

My girlfriend Lydia was with me as with a degree of nervous anticipation we drove up to the house. Our first impressions were positive if a little scary. There were piglets and snowdrops in abundance. Snowdrops, probably my favourite flowers, seemed to bloom everywhere and the little piglets scampered around the orchard next to the house, and seemingly wherever else their fancy took them.

What an introduction. How could you not love a house with piglets and snowdrops? And that was just the start. There were farm buildings, cow byres, a big barn, a crew yard with calves munching hay, that unique farmyard smell and best of all a small river or beck, a water mill adjacent to the house and rushing water just outside the kitchen window.

I was transfixed, wide eyed. To live somewhere like this was beyond my wildest dreams. I had no ambition to earn my living from farming and in any case had long been part of an established family engineering business, but my imagination ran riot. The potential for experiencing a truly rural life in such an interesting and countrified location seemed almost irresistible.

Wilf, the farmer, a widower who had occupied the house and farmed the land for forty years greeted us at the door with a welcoming smile and invited us in to enjoy a cup of coffee by the fire. This was the 'icing on the cake'. His warm reception and the friendly atmosphere was immediately relaxing and although the interior was simple and shall we say basic in a way which perhaps suited an old working farmhouse, we could not help but allow our thoughts to stray to how amazing it could be

I felt even more at home when I realised that the fireplace we were sitting by was exactly the same as one in the house I grew up in, evidently built by the same local builder who did work for my parents and who later was to become hugely helpful to me.

At this time the auction had not even been advertised which I think gave me an advantage over any competition, of which I was sure there would be plenty. It was also encouraging to learn that Wilf knew of my family. My parents lived in the nearby village for a number of years after they were married, and even though they had since moved away, an aunt lived quite near and my father's old family home was only a few miles away.

Indeed, I was able to get in ahead of the field so to speak due to a visit with my parents the previous Christmas to see their old friend Jack, who with his family farmed locally.

Sitting around their cosy log fire after tea, Jack, knowing I was in the market for a country property said 'You don't fancy a spot of fishing do you?' He then went on to tell me that Wilf was shortly to retire and that the farm was coming up for sale. He even said that there used to be otters there years ago.

Well I didn't need to hear any more. This was at a time when otters were extremely scarce and I had never seen one!

To attempt to buy the farm was however still a big step, and I was anxious to arrange another visit to view the property, and hopefully gain a second opinion from the family. This time I was accompanied by my brother Nigel and sister-in-law Nicki who both came along to see what I was threatening to buy, as well as to give me moral support. Having parked the car way upstream we walked down river towards the water mill intending to have a look around without bothering Wilf. But as luck would have it we were overtaken by a violent thunder storm.

It came up with little warning and the rain was torrential. We had nowhere to shelter and had no alternative but to run back towards the car which was a good half mile away, and abandon our viewing. The lightning was intense and incessant and we were lucky to avoid being struck. By the time we reached the car we were literally soaked to the skin.

There followed an uncomfortable drive home in Nicki's Morris Minor and we never got to see the mill or the farmhouse.

Was the storm and the wetting a bad omen? Only time would tell.

A Page from the Diary

April 15th 2006

Dull start, still. *Moorhen nest building front of mill, Gt Spotted Woodpecker on 'leader' of second fir tree behind house, Goldfinches visiting nest site top of first fir tree.* *Gt Spotted Woodpecker 'drumming' loudly, Green Woodpecker 'laughing', Kestrel calling 'mating cry', Shellduck flying from quarry area.* *Bumble bees active.* *Blackbirds singing am.* *First Blackcap song.* *Squirrels making huge leap across river (from tree to tree), only just able to make the distance.* *Willow Warblers singing.* *Four Mallard drakes on water (pm), duck brooding eggs.* *Oyster Catcher (first one this spring) flying around calling early eve.* *Lovely warm late afternoon.* *Barn Owl (female) flew to nesting barn 8.05 pm (daylight), then set off hunting over rape fields, hedgerows towards Trent.* *Approx. quarter hour later male entered barn then flew off hunting along fields adjacent to drive.* *Must have young in nest.* *Pippistrelle flying over barn field.*

A Page from the Diary

May 28th 2016

Lovely morning, brilliant sunshine after misty start, very warm.   Pair of Pied Wagtails appear to have taken up residence.   Buzzard, driven away by Carrion Crows as usual, over wood near drive. (am)   Pied Wagtails nest building in honeysuckle in back yard.   Jay scolding (a roosting owl?) edge of orchard.   Barn Owl hunting approx. 9am, bright sunshine, flew through orchard and later over barn field. Buzzard again overhead, again seen off by Carrion Crow. Chiffchaffs and Blackbirds singing loudly. Mistle Thrush singing early. Eve. Mallard duck with nine tiny ducklings on water.

CHAPTER II
A New Life Beckons

Well the sale came and went. I did not attend the auction myself. I thought that I would have a better chance of success if the matter was in the hands of a professional. So it was that Robert a good friend and chartered surveyor who had already looked at the property for me, did the bidding on my behalf.

What a strange day that was. I went about my business as usual but it seemed impossible to concentrate on anything other than the auction. Finally, at about 3.30 in the afternoon I received the call which told me that my bid had been successful. I must confess that at first I did not know whether to be glad or sorry, as the full realisation and the ultimate challenge of ownership hit me.

I had not only bought a house, but a farm and a water mill! Who has their own water mill for goodness sake?

This was the start of a new era and there could be no backing down. I knew I must deal with a host of new problems and responsibilities. At first it seemed a daunting prospect, but any negative thoughts were soon dismissed and the practical side of my nature coupled with a determination to succeed, whatever the odds, eventually kicked in.

But, would I be able to handle the work necessary to manage the property? Could I afford to make the necessary improvements to the house and outbuildings to ensure that life would be acceptably comfortable and practical in this relatively remote location?

Then there was the issue of security. Who would look after the place when I could not be there? Would the river flood and what about all the rats that lived in the mill?

I had a few weeks to consider these matters, which probably did not help, while waiting for Wilf to vacate the house and move to a new address in the village. At last the day came when I could first drive over those bumps and hollows in the long stony track as the 'owner' and rightful occupant, and I must admit to feeling a little nervous at that moment, as well as something of an interloper. The piglets had gone, and the calves, and the snowdrops had long been over as it was now mid summer.

With Lydia I wandered somewhat aimlessly around recognising afresh the size of the challenge which lay ahead. There were two very small kittens which appeared to have been left behind, one black and white and one ginger, black and white and we fed them in the little back yard by the water and thought of the future and how beautiful it could all be one day.

The house came with five and a half acres of land which included about a quarter mile stretch of the river, known locally as the beck, with fishing rights, a garden, a field, two orchards, all the farm buildings and the water mill. It was a lot to take in, where would I start?

During that first long hot summer I worked hard, mostly outdoors, removing old fences, trees, undergrowth and anything which I thought would get in the way of my long term vision. Meanwhile plans were in hand and planning permission sought for improvements to the house but it would be another twelve months and a bit more before I was able to move in.

One day clearing undergrowth with my father on the river bank behind the mill we discovered a second stream, a waterfall and sluice completely covered in brambles and nettles so as to be almost invisible.

This was a notable find and turned out to be an overflow channel, designed to bypass the mill race at times of high water.   It now runs free, water tumbles over the fall continuously and fish venture in to the lower reaches.

As time went by we spent more and more time at the farm, working both in and out of the house and generally following my dream. The kittens had mysteriously disappeared by this time and we could only think that they may have been taken by a fox which had an earth nearby in the river bank. We hoped not but we never saw them again.

Shortly afterwards Lydia and I parted company, and I wondered how I would cope, if necessary on my own, in these exciting but as yet unfamiliar surroundings.

The answer would come with the richness and diversity of the events and experiences which were yet to unfold. Gradually the fascination and interest in my surroundings together with the extraordinary wildlife I was to encounter on a daily basis reignited my passion and enthusiasm.

I had been introduced to a firm of architects who helped with the planning and design for the initial alterations to the interior of the house. These included the conversion of two sunken pantries into an extended hallway and utility room, the creation of a good sized drawing room from an area that originally contained a coal house and outside toilet, and the connection by landing of two formerly independent stairways.

In the course of this work original beams were exposed and I spent many very cold and tiring hours cleaning these and scraping off the previous covering of whitewash. This was painstaking and dirty work which occupied many a winter afternoon, but I recall that commentaries of Nottingham Forest football matches (they were doing rather well in those days) and listening to Abba records on my portable radio helped to pass the time!

It was winter and the daylight hours were short. Often in semi darkness I had to work with makeshift lighting. I remember I felt very isolated, but at the same time excited and content, as I looked forward to the future and the many opportunities which might lay ahead.

A Page from the Diary

Another lovely sunny morning.   Two pairs of Tufted duck on the water for a while, also pair of Mallard.   Common Blue, Orange Tip and Brimstone butterflies in the garden, along with 'Cabbage' Whites.   Very warm day.   Blackcap singing around orchard (pm).   Sparrow Hawk overhead.   Buttercups starting to come in 'ha ha' field, also some 'Ladies Smock'.   Loud shriek from behind the house (pm), a Carrion Crow diving on and chasing off a Heron, just above the river.   The crow then had the audacity to perch on the mill roof, where it was immediately the target of the Jackdaws which dived on it continually until it moved away.

A Page from the Diary

June 12th 2016

Overcast but fine start.   Kingfisher with fish in it's beak on back yard wall (am).   Flew low upstream when disturbed by aerial 'games' overhead involving Carrion Crow and a host of 'dive bombing' Jackdaws.   River flowing strongly after rain.   Goldcrests singing from yew trees, also Chaffinch.   Tufted duck flying around making distinctive 'quacking' call, unlike other ducks.   More rain lunchtime onwards.   Blackcaps around garden area, think they are feeding young, Chiffchaff singing, also Blackbirds and Mistle Thrush (early) Stoat on bridleway, also baby rabbits… sure the Stoat will get a good meal!   Oyster Catchers flying around 'piping' loudly.

CHAPTER III

A View From The Window

Eventually came the day when I was able to move in, and day to day life at the farm soon proved to be something of a revelation, the experience being even more rewarding than anything I could have imagined. I still clearly remember the first night, feeling truly alone and yet comforted by the feel of the house, the sound of the water rushing past and the novelty of a dark but starlit sky little affected by artificial light.

The nearest neighbour was about half a mile away, there were no near roads and I recall the silence was only broken by the sound of water and the cries of lapwings flying overhead.

The next morning I awoke to find tree sparrows around the mill and mallard ducks and moorhens on the water. The kitchen windows looked both up and down stream, the water flowing by almost within touching distance, and as the days went on I would witness the most remarkable sights from these viewpoints.

Kingfishers became almost an everyday happening, their electric blue plumage flashing in the sun as they flew low over the water uttering their piercing whistle like calls. Frequently they fish from the back yard wall, diving spectacularly within a few feet of the window. They also perch on the wires under the footbridge just downstream of the mill, or on waterside bushes and trees, always providing me with a grandstand view of their fishing skills.

One winter a kingfisher regularly roosted on some bare branches which grew out over the water just in front of the house. At night when the trees were encrusted with white frost, it looked like a brilliantly coloured Christmas bauble, illuminated by the flood light on the mill bridge.

Herons are a constant source of interest. These birds are frequently seen from the windows, wading in the water or standing on the banks, and always alert and ready to jab their spear like beaks into the water in order to catch and swallow whole their prey.

I have watched them fishing within three or four yards of the house and even perched on the back yard wall. Sometimes I get home in the late afternoon or early evening to find a heron standing sentinel like on the grassy river bank as though on guard, overseeing all before it.

Fish, frogs, and sometimes voles feature in their diet, but on one occasion I observed from my kitchen the consumption of a good sized rat. The rat I remember represented a considerable challenge and the bird struggled to get the animal down its throat, which distended hugely, only to disgorge it later and then swallow it again. These efforts were repeated over a period of about half an hour before success was achieved, after which the bird rested for some considerable time before finally taking flight.

Grey wagtails arrive most years about March and serenade me with their sweet song as they flit and bounce around the back yard, their bright yellow underparts, black bibs and constantly wagging tails always catching the eye. Remarkably they often nest quite close to the window, either on a ledge in the mill race or in the ivy clad mill wall. When fledged their chicks adorn my yard and tile roofs as they learn to fly and are fed by their parents.

All the time the river rushes by. A pair of mallard come every spring with the intention of nesting either under ferns on the river bank or in the ivy on the mill roof, but the duck can never make up her mind. Every morning for weeks it seems in February or March the pair float down towards the mill race and the duck then proceeds to explore the possibilities for a nest site. She makes an enormous fuss about flying up into the ivy on the mill roof and walks or scrabbles about in it for ages while the drake waits patiently on the water, or on the back yard wall quietly quacking or chasing off rival drakes. Then she flies down and goes through the whole procedure again, investigating the ground cover on the bank.

This can go on for some days but she eventually decides on a site, eggs are laid and in most years eight or ten little yellow and brown ducklings arrive on the water closely shepherded by their mother, while the drake keeps a somewhat disinterested distance.

How can I be so lucky to see all this from my kitchen window? Stoats, foxes, bats and squirrels regularly appear together with other water birds including moorhens, tufted ducks, smart little teal and gadwall ducks, on a couple of occasions a mute swan and her cygnets, and graceful pure white egrets, relatives of the heron family which hunt for fish and invertebrates in the shallows.

The swan brought her brood to my back yard on a number of occasions and they came so close I could almost have touched them, but I wondered how the adult would manage to 'take off' from such a comparatively restricted area of water should it need to do so. Maybe she walked back to the lake from whence she came?

The tufted ducks arrive every spring, about May time, and nest under the umbrella like leaves of butterbur or amongst the tall grass and water plants by the water's edge. The drakes look immaculate in their black and white plumage and the birds frequently dive for food, as is their habit, even in the comparatively shallow water of the beck.

Water voles lived in the river banks within yards of the house in the early years and could be seen 'plopping' in and out of the water and swimming back and forth between the banks. A water rail scuttled from a patch of reeds on one occasion and in very cold weather coots and even a little grebe or dabchick have appeared.

Other remarkable sightings have included visiting redshank, greenshank and green sandpiper, all wading birds attracted by shallow water downstream during early spring months, and again in full view from the window.

Oyster catchers, those black and white wading birds with red legs and red beaks, which for the rest of the year frequent sea shores and estuaries, can be seen flying over in spring and early summer. Their piping calls carry far and wide, and from early autumn and into the winter months the local greylag geese fly low overhead virtually every day.

One day I heard loud screaming from just outside the rear window and saw a male sparrow hawk on the surface of the water holding a starling in its talons for some minutes and appearing to try and drown it. I have never heard of this behaviour before and cannot be certain that this was its intention but it certainly appeared to be the case. The hawk eventually flew off carrying the starling which I think was still alive.

Once a fox caught and killed a young rabbit in the back yard and trotted off with the unfortunate victim in its jaws.

It was from the kitchen window that I learned that juvenile moorhens from a first nest will sometimes help their parents feeding and brooding the chicks from a second clutch. Behaviour I would think probably unique to moorhens, I witnessed this at close range several times, a nest being situated within a few yards of my window, close to where the water tumbled from the mill race.

Conversely I have watched on other occasions adult moorhens displaying hostile behaviour to young birds from an earlier brood, and even attacking them. Feisty and unpredictable birds are moorhens!

Barn, tawny and little owls I have watched from my kitchen many times, and even buzzards. I remember once during a cold spell in winter a little owl took to roosting in a small ivy covered tree just behind the coal house and stared at me with wide open eyes as I stood at the kitchen sink.

Almost every day seems to bring something new and I never tire of the ever changing scene. Talk about a room with a view!

A Page from the Diary

May 21st 2006

Dull start, rain by mid morning.   Goldcrests busy around fir trees

(prob nesting).   Moorhens on water near their nest.   Mistle

thrush (scolding) early again.   Lots of buttercups in 'ha ha' field

and barn fields, may blossom fully out (white), lilac fully out also.

Six or seven Moorhen chicks out in field (in wet grass) with their

parents. Unusual as chicks very small and vulnerable.   Pair of

Shelduck flying around, three Mallard drakes on water behind mill.

Raining most of the day.   Pheasants and Rabbits in 'ha ha' field

amongst the buttercups, Blackcap and Willow warbler singing,

Bullfinches 'piping' in hedges, Chaffinches active.   Adult Heron

fishing below bridge, mid afternoon.   Six or seven ducklings on water

beyond bridge with their mother.   Pair of Tufted ducks on water

behind mill, early eve. Interestingly last year saw a pair on the 16th

May.

A Page from the Diary

August 21st 2016

Bright start, less windy, just a breeze.   A Raven flew over approx. 9am, a deep croak heralded its presence, followed by four more (very loud croaks) as it flew low over the house heading upstream.   Mallard duck and two half grown ducklings on water front of mill (pm), 'dabbling' in the weed.   Moorhens behind the mill.   (pm) Painted Lady butterfly (my favourite) in yard garden around buddleja.   Also Red   Admiral   and   Small   Tortoiseshell   but   only   odd numbers......nothing like the quantity of other years.   But the Painted Lady was a bonus!

CHAPTER IV
A Thousand Campers

This is not a chapter or a title one expects to find in a book largely devoted to wild life and the countryside, but as I recall and tell the story of some of the more notable events and influences on my life in this country retreat, the annual arrival of a host of camping enthusiasts is difficult to ignore

Nobody told me I would be inundated with weekend campers and caravaners every twelve months, but to my astonishment this is exactly what happened in the October of my first year, when the pastures immediately adjacent to my property were turned into a virtual town overnight. A vast array of canvas, caravans, cars and trucks were positioned, stretching in neat lines for nearly half a mile in any direction from my boundary and within fifty yards or so of the house. My normally quiet and remote location was suddenly alive with campers, walkers, children and dogs!

On waking and looking out of my bedroom window one Saturday morning and witnessing the camp for the first time I could not believe my eyes. Instead of fields, hedges and trees I could see nothing but caravans. Suddenly I had literally hundreds of neighbours! My world was transformed.

As the day progressed loud speaker announcements by the organisers came drifting on the breeze, and these continued throughout the day and in to the evening. I soon became well informed regarding the camp and all the activities which were being organised. There were games and competitions for the children and even a beauty contest. I seem to remember the winner was crowned 'Miss Maid Marian', in recognition of the local legend of Robin Hood and nearby Sherwood Forest!

Minding my own business, and looking somewhat scruffy and unkempt to any passing campers, most of whom probably thought I was the gardener or caretaker, I tried to ignore what was going on over the hedge. But there was the smell from cooking and camping stoves, dogs barking, music played over the sound system in between announcements from the organisers, and to cap it all scores of balloons which were released and found their way in to my garden and surrounding fields.

It was all a total culture shock for me, and something I was completely unprepared for! No doubt my friends and family found it all very amusing, knowing my liking for privacy and even solitude, but the funny side was lost on me.

I was stuck with a virtual holiday camp in my space and there was absolutely nothing I could do about it.

On making enquiries I later found out that anything up to a thousand people (or was it a thousand caravans?) were occupying the site having travelled from all parts of the country, some indeed from as far away as Cornwall! It transpired that the gathering constituted a traditional meet of a national camping and caravan club which was timed to coincide with Nottingham's famous Goose Fair. The campers arrived on the Friday and departed on the Sunday afternoon.

I should have suspected something was amiss when I saw my neighbouring farmer using a mechanical digger to create troughs and pits in the ground just the other side of my boundary fence several days before the event. These turned out to be latrines for the camp site, although I did not know that at the time. I thought this rather inconsiderate, bearing in mind the close proximity to my land, but I have to admit that once the caravans had left, the ground was fully restored and the site comprehensively cleared of all litter.

I distinctly remember the feeling of inner joy and contentment when they had gone however, and thinking how lucky I was to live here all the time, whereas the 'visitors' could only enjoy the place for a few days. They don't come any more. They moved to an alternative site after only three or four years, much to my relief, but looking back, having to share my private world with hundreds of strangers, even for a short period, was probably quite character building. Although way out of my comfort zone, the presence of the campers was something that in the end I learnt to live with, in spite of my initial reaction to the 'invasion'. I even managed to be civil to them when passing the time of day as they walked their dogs on the bridle way!

Having returned home very late one night, during one of the camping weekends I walked across to look at the caravans before going to bed. There was a brilliant moon and a clear sky, all was calm and silent and the inhabitants presumably retired for the night. The moonlight reflected on the van roofs and the white canvas and I must admit to a certain fascination, keeping watch as it were in the small hours while hundreds slept. There was something about being wide awake, under the moon and the stars, on 'my patch' with all those sleeping souls completely unaware of my presence.

What effect did the arrival of the caravans and the sprawling camp site have on the local wild life? The answer to this question was, remarkably, very little. Kingfishers still flew up and down stream, their piercing whistles competing with the sounds from the camp, and herons still came down to fish in the evenings when the occupants of the camp were elsewhere. Moorhens and ducks frequented the water behind the mill where it was quieter, kestrels hunted over the adjacent fields and tawny owls still 'hooted' during the dark hours in spite of the near by 'sea' of unfamiliar lights.

The badgers and foxes were forced to find different foraging grounds, their regular routes being blocked by big shiny vans and tents, but they could travel anywhere they pleased and would not go short of a meal. The many rabbits had to find plants to nibble in fresh fields but it was only for three days and they would still be running around long after the visitors had gone. When the big marquee was taken down and the caravans and motor homes had departed, the land returned to normal. Cattle were reintroduced, the grass grew fresh and green again and I enjoyed the knowledge that it would be a whole year before the scenario was acted out again.

Looking back it all seems like a distant dream, or was it a nightmare? At least thirty years have passed since the 'Goose Fair Camp' last came. The outlook is green all year round now, the only occupants of the former site being a large flock of sheep, and of course the many wild things for which the fields, trees and hedges are home. Long may it be so.

A Page from the Diary

Overcast start (again), but calmer. Woodpecker 'drumming'. A sure sign of spring! Pair of Grey Wagtails around water, front of mill. Twelve Whooper Swans flying high to north east, calling to each other, audible even at such a height! Green Woodpecker 'yaffling' during morning. Two Buzzards soaring over yard garden. Later Peregrine Falcon high overhead and calling continuously, pursued by a Buzzard! (am) Beautiful warm, sunny afternoon! Watched three Buzzards from kitchen window, two low over trees behind house. One of them dived on a Jackdaw but didn't catch it. Not seen that before! The Buzzard dived and twisted through the trees in effort to catch the Jackdaw. Fieldfares still around.

A Page from the Diary

April 3rd 2015

Dull, drizzly start but calm.   Buzzard gliding over house early.

Grey Wagtails and Mallard about.   Large flock of Black Headed

Gulls swirling round and round calling excitedly, directly overhead.

Not sure why, doesn't seem warm enough for a concentration of insects.

Coal Tit with other tits on nut feeder.   Dead (and largely eaten)

Jackdaw on ground near weeping ash.   Two Egrets standing in 'ha

ha' field, preening their feathers, absolutely 'snow white'.   Song thrush

singing (pm), also Blackbirds and Chiffchaff.   Also Great tits,

Chaffinches, Robins and Green Woodpecker 'yaffling'.   Continuous

drizzle all day.   Stoat in front garden (pm), very bright chestnut and

white, with black tipped tail.

CHAPTER V

Groundworks

In due course I was able to divert my energies once again to the many tasks still awaiting attention in the grounds, the house and the outbuildings.

One of the first jobs was to deal with a deep well. Overgrown and out of use for many years, it was not only untidy but potentially dangerous so I felt it should be filled in. This was achieved by tipping in rubble left by the builders from the work carried out on the house, removing the rockery which surrounded it, and seeding the ground so as to convert the site in to part of the lawn.

The well seemed to go down for ever, there was water at the bottom, it was about four feet diameter and lined with specially made curved bricks. I have often wondered what the water was used for and why it was even necessary, bearing in mind the close presence of the river, and in retrospect sometimes regret getting rid of it. Another piece of history after all, like the mill, the bread oven, the copper and the old lead pumps in what is now my dining room.

A large Irish yew tree grew in the middle of the lawn which blocked out much of the light from the front rooms, and I felt, spoiled the view of the house. I always think this variety of yew suggests an atmosphere of a churchyard, which for some reason I was not entirely happy about. The tree was obviously of considerable age and I am not entirely sure I should have felled it, but without giving the matter too much thought I decided to remove it myself.

This was seriously hard work, especially when it came to digging out the roots, but the result very favourably changed the aspect, improved the light, and looking back I think was well worth the effort. It is too late to worry now, but I hope it didn't have a preservation order on it!

Perhaps to ease my conscience I subsequently planted several English yews around the garden, which together with two large and quite impressive existing examples helped I thought to repay my debt to society, if not to the Irish!

A larger undertaking, for which I required assistance, was the construction of a ha ha behind the house. I had taken a hedge out along the edge of a ditch thereby providing an ideal site, and the ha ha was to provide a barrier to livestock without obstructing the view across the field.

Cyril (Cyd) my builder friend who made the fireplace and who was still working into his eighties and early nineties, constructed the sunken wall, while I obtained twenty tons of earth to infill behind it. Unfortunately, this was dumped a fair distance from where it was required and I rather foolishly decided that I would move the soil myself by wheelbarrow.

It was wet weather, the ground consequently very soft and instead of moving a little at a time I took as much as the barrow would hold on every trip. My back has felt it ever since. I can't remember the number of journeys I made but I think I seriously underestimated the task, and its effect on my body!

To add insult to injury, it wasn't too long before some of the sheep learnt to jump over the ha ha on to the lawn. The answer to this problem was to erect low railings along the edge, which whilst not detracting from the visual effect, certainly stopped the leaping sheep.

There is an old 'weeping' ash tree at the side of the house, just by the ha ha, which when I first came here was like a huge living umbrella. During those early days when the house was undergoing alteration I sometimes ate my picnic lunch under this tree, listening to a chiffchaff singing in its upper branches and marvelling that I was completely sheltered, even from quite heavy rain showers.

I thought it was a willow at first, until I noticed that its branches were bare right into the second half of May. The penny dropped then of course, but I hadn't realised before that a weeping variety of ash even existed.

The old tree has lost some large limbs since then and no longer has quite that umbrella effect. The trunk and some of the remaining branches are partly hollow and have provided homes in recent years for nesting jackdaws, and once a pair of little owls.

In early spring the ground underneath is decorated by a carpet of snowdrops and golden yellow aconites. But it was not always so. When I first arrived the ground was heavily contaminated by soot. Evidently Wilf had allowed his chimney sweep to dump excess soot in this spot for years. Maybe though, the presence of soot in the soil acts as a fertiliser, judging by the prolific spread of the bulbs since that time?

Meanwhile, over by the farmyard the Dutch barn was demolished, the crew yard converted in to a garden and a cow byre into a cottage. All this work was spread out over a number of years, along with repairs to the mill and further improvements to the house.

About this time and following some unusually severe winter conditions I noticed a number of brown stains on the bedroom ceilings. On investigation it transpired that these were caused by snow blowing through the gaps in the roof tiles and melting on the plaster between the rafters.

The existing roof was in fact no better insulated than a barn, the wind blowing right through the tiles. To cure the problem the entire roof had to be stripped and felted in order to keep out the snow and also to prevent the water pipes from freezing.

The job was undertaken by Cyd who even in his advanced years was happy to erect scaffolding and work at heights which would certainly scare me. This was invaluable and the work should have been carried out earlier, had I realised the problems which could arise. The pipes in the loft had already frozen once and I definitely did not like the stains on the ceilings!

The crew yard which was full of muck, straw and calves when I first saw it, became a sheltered garden with pathways, shrubs and perennials, including a herb garden. Full of colours, butterflies and the scent of lavender, and shielded from the winds by the surrounding barns and stables, the garden has become a favourite retreat on warm summer days. Indeed, even in winter it can be an effective 'sun trap,' and provides an attractive amenity to the cottage.

Sunflowers were planted here one year, and during an evening in the pub, encouraged by the convivial atmosphere and a certain amount of alcohol, I boasted that my sunflowers would grow taller than those being grown at her home by a very keen gardener friend, Sarah, who I knew to be very competitive.

It must have been the beer talking but having once publicly issued the challenge, and being equally competitive myself, the prospect of losing the contest was not an option.

I had never grown sunflowers before but the sheltered and sunlit garden evidently suited them, or was it the trace of manure from the cow yard still in the ground? Either way the plants grew big and strong and reached at least seven feet high. Sarah could not compete with this and I must admit to enjoying my moment of triumph, even if the location and the manure did give me a somewhat unfair advantage! The flower heads were the size of dinner plates. It's amazing what a little cow muck can do!

Over the years I managed to acquire more land from neighbouring farmers. Many trees have been planted forming small wooded areas, orchards extended and pasture added creating a mosaic of habitat for wildlife as well as an 'oasis' of countryside, more akin to that which I knew and loved as a child rather than the working farm I started with.

Of course it was always a possibility that being an ancient site any excavations or changes to land use might one day turn up something of value. I used to kid myself that I might find a bag of golden sovereigns, or perhaps a medieval sword in the bottom of the river, after all who knows what might be lurking in the depths.

Carol, my secretary and p.a. in the engineering business, stayed with her husband in the cottage once or twice to 'house sit' while I was away on holiday and took advantage of the opportunity to pursue their interest in metal detecting. However, in spite of the fact that successive owners have occupied the site since the time of the Doomsday Book I do not believe anything was ever found. At least not that they admitted to!

I may be able to claim rights to buried treasure should anything of significance ever come to light, but something that was said many years ago often comes back to me.

Roger who was very involved in the early alterations to the house and produced much of the joinery work, was very interested in the mill and its workings and the history of the place, but he pointed out that although technically I was the owner, I was in reality merely a caretaker or custodian of the property as long as I lived here.

He was right, I can`t take it with me when I go, but my adventure in the meantime was well underway.

A Page from the Diary

May 15th 2005

Brilliant day. Warm and sunny. Mallard duck and four ducklings on water with drake in attendance.   Grey Wagtail on back yard wall.   Fox cub in wood 'face to face' with me three/four yards away... not afraid.   Young Tawny Owl calling from nest box? In wood.   Green woodpecker calling 'laughing'.   Stoat crossed gravel by ford.   Willow warblers singing from plantations. Sand Martins and Swallows overhead. Two Herons fly low over barns and meadow at dusk.   Many Bats hunting along drive.   Kestrel roosting on barn.   Red legged Partridges calling.   Barn Owl flying low from barn to go hunting (flying north) 9.30 pm.

A Page from the Diary

Sunny start to day. Pair of Grey Wagtails around back yard, very

active.   Blue Tits still frantically feeding young in air vent. Hope

they don't get too big to get out?   Moorhen and chicks in

shallows beyond bridge.   Bullfinches 'piping', Blackbirds,

Chaffinches singing.   Kestrel hovering over hay meadow behind

ha ha… golden with buttercups.   Willow warblers singing in

plantations.   Swallows investigating coal house.

Dreamy afternoon.   Sand Martins racing about the sky, calling

constantly…comforting somehow.   Fox cub 'stalking' large cock

Pheasant in hay meadow behind ha ha…not a very even contest (in the

Pheasant's favour).   Song thrush singing early eve.   Heron

flying in over hay meadow to fish in river (eve).   Yellow Hammers

(pair) near drive, also Linnets, Bullfinch and Green Woodpecker

'laughing' from oak tree.

CHAPTER VI
The Seasons

Today the sheep arrived. It must be spring, but then I knew that when the first chiffchaff sang from the still bare branches of the hazels in the nut grove behind the orchard. The apple trees, some of them ancient and twisted with age carry swelling buds promising glorious spring blossom and the tinkling song of goldfinches to come. But the chiffchaff, generally the first of the migrant birds to reach these shores having successfully completed a hazardous journey from Africa, happily braves the still cold air and pours out its simple song, a prelude to the full orchestration to come.

It is the end of March, the equinox is already behind us and the days are now at least as long as the nights. Frost still deposits its tiny ice crystals on the grass in the meadow, only to melt away sooner each day as the sun brings a fragile warmth to the land, but the sheep don't mind.

The grass has a springtime fresh green to it and the ewes have already explored their new territory, followed closely be their tiny lambs which in a few days time, at around sunset, will be running races and charging around like boisterous children. Even the ewes join in, somewhat reluctantly, on occasions. Sometimes a fox will cross the field and observe the fun and games but neither the sheep nor the fox show any more than mild curiosity to each other.

The winter thrushes, the bold fieldfares and their gentler redwing companions, have already left on their long journey back to northern lands and their summer territory, perhaps guided by those green shafts of light which penetrate the vast arctic skies, and which so fascinate we humans.

I must confess I miss them at first. The 'chuckling' cries of the fieldfares and the 'seep' calls of the redwings as they fly overhead in ragged restless groups against a grey sky, or invade the orchard seeking the food provided by the many fallen apples, is something I get very used to during the winter months and it seems strangely quiet for a time when they have gone.

Such events contribute to a heightening of the senses and an appreciation of the changing seasons. It is noticeable how much more aware we are of the gradual turning or advancement of the year and the rhythms of life, when in a truly rural environment.

The farming activities which surround us tell the same tale. The progress of winter or autumn sown crops, the green of the grass, the trimming of hedges, the ploughing, the harvest, and the presence of lambs or calves in the fields all clearly illustrate the changing seasons.

When April comes we look for the return of the swallows which invariably come back to the barn, porch or garage in which they nested the previous year. Their close cousins the sand martins normally arrive well ahead of the swallows and are followed by house martins but how any of them manage to navigate thousands of miles back to where they started life is one of nature's true wonders.

April 20th was the date around which the cuckoo used to arrive, but alas this bird is heard only rarely in these parts nowadays, as is the case with the turtle dove, which used to croon gently in the thorn hedges throughout the summer months. Many warblers still come however, and this time of the year the air is filled with the song of chiffchaffs, willow warblers, blackcaps and whitethroats, adding their voices to the more familiar resident chorus of garden birds.

Common terns or 'sea swallows' reappear to dance about the sky, making an interesting addition to the usual black headed and lesser black backed gulls which seem to be present all year. Brightly coloured oyster catchers come back to nest by the local gravel pits and announce their presence by their shrill calls. Later when they have young these birds can frequently be seen carrying worms in their long beaks as they fly back from their feeding grounds.

Nesting is now in full swing in the bird world. The rooks have been busy repairing their old residences since February, herons and tawny owls also will have made early starts and now every bird in the air, from ducks to finches and thrushes will be either nest building or laying their eggs.

The first bright green leaves appear on the hawthorns in early March, followed by the blackthorn blossom and later the may flowers. The apple, pear, and cherry trees flower, the daffodils, primroses, violets and bluebells bloom and when the sky is blue everything is all right with the world.

Bright golden celandines in the bottom of the hedgerows seem to reflect the early warmth of the sun and a buzzard soaring high above on broad wings `mewing` to its mate completes the scene. And if you listen carefully, a faint and tremulous song from above reveals a skylark climbing higher and higher into the blue, until almost invisible to the naked eye.

Bumble bees drone about, enjoying the early sunshine and the spring flowers. They make nests in abandoned mouse holes in the soft ground or crevices in rotting or fallen trees.

The catkins are prominent on the hazel bushes and alders, and blue tits and newly arrived warblers hunt among them for insects. 'Lamb's tails', the hazel wands are sometimes called, and although they formed during the winter it is only when spring comes that they show their gentle primrose yellow colouring as they wave in the breeze.

Fresh leaves now adorn many of the trees. Following hard on the heels of the hawthorns the chestnuts, alders, hazel and maple burst in to leaf, and together with all the other trees and shrubs combine to create a new green world to welcome the incoming summer.

The very last trees to gain a coat of green are the ash and the oak, some of which are still bare until well into May, or even on occasions early June! At this time I often think of the old saying 'if the oak is out before the ash, we're only going to get a splash' and conversely 'if the ash is out before the oak we're surely going to get a soak', referring of course to rainfall to come, or lack of it! Summer is full of butterflies, wild flowers in the meadow, damsel and dragonflies over the water and the scent of hay. High flying swifts scream in the sky, swallows skim the water and the fields, and wood pigeons 'coo' on warm afternoons.

Wild flowers were planted in what used to be arable land behind the ha ha and beside the bridle way some years past and they are now a riot of colour from May to August. The buttercups are the first to bloom and form a shimmering golden carpet, augmented in time by ladies smock, corn cockle, clover, vetch, white daisies, plantains, knapweed, birds foot trefoil, or 'eggs and bacon' as we used to call it, and many other flowering plants and grasses including a few spotted or common orchids.

Red campion and ragged robin bloom everywhere, and even cowslips flourish around the garden edges where they are undisturbed. Tall foxgloves and valerian grow wherever they can gain a foothold, whilst water celandines and luxurious yellow kingcups decorate the water's edge in sheltered spots

The butterflies and the bees love the flower meadow, and meadow brown, small coppers, common blues and many others whose names I cannot recall, take wing as I walk through the dew covered grasses and herbs which make up a kaleidoscope of colours, especially on a bright summer morning. Every bird in the air sings and baby rabbits are everywhere.

In the garden small tortoiseshell, red admiral and peacock butterflies dominate, together with orange tips and brimstones in the early summer. When the buddleja flowers their ranks are joined by commas with their curiously shaped wings and, in a really special year, by lovely tawny orange, black and white painted ladies. These are my favourites, and have braved often wild seas and hundreds of miles over land to reach our gardens.

Towards the end of July, when the wild flowers have had a chance to spread their seed, Andy the hay cutter arrives with his huge tractor and mows all the long grass in the fields which the sheep have not yet grazed.

I used to have the hay baled, and I remember the bales looked and smelled amazing lying in the freshly cut fields. One night under a big moon I walked out after dark and sat on a pile of bales in the middle of a field for some time, contemplating the rural scene and drinking in the scent of the grass. As far as the eye could see, the fields, some of them being harvested, and the hedges and trees lit by moonlight stretched in every direction. It was magical, serene, yet a little mysterious, and I was the only spectator! It made me feel very privileged, content and a bit like a real farmer!

My original plan was to sell the bales to the horse fraternity, initially with some success, but I finished up selling them one at a time to people with pet rabbits! This was just not worth the effort at £1 a bale and became a bit trying, but the real problem came when I had the bales stored in the big barn.

The bales may not have been quite dry enough when they were stacked and after a while became very warm in the middle. I feared they might have caught fire and set light to the barn if I did not spread them out to dry.

Dismantling a hay stack is heavy work and did nothing for the state of my back, so the following year I decided that baling was not worth either the labour involved or the worry, unless I could dispose of them in one lot, straight from the fields. It did not help either that I could see from the evidence of comparatively new brickwork on parts of the barn, and an obvious re roofing job, that the building had likely been on fire at some time in the past.

I now leave the cut grass where it lies and it is gradually absorbed by the earth or eaten by the sheep which are introduced shortly afterwards.

The oncoming of autumn is predicted as early as August by the local grey lag and canada geese which start to flock and fly over the house in ever increasing numbers through to September, into October and beyond. These are resident birds living in the Trent valley throughout the year and not to be confused with the truly wild flocks which from time to time, during the winter months, appear on their migration.

The local geese nevertheless make a great spectacle as they come over in V formation, usually at fairly low height, clamouring loudly on their way to and from their roosts on local disused gravel pits. They remind me of squadrons of low flying aircraft, and curiously, sometimes have a pure white bird towards the front of their formation.

A couple of times a large flock has descended on the field immediately behind the house, which I call the 'ha ha' field. They stayed on the ground for an hour or two and covered a large part of the field. So much so that the sheep which were grazing there had to retire to the edges, being unwilling to compete with a hundred or so noisy geese. Eventually they all took wing, almost as one, leaving the sheep to graze in peace once again.

Meantime, the harvest has been gathered in the surrounding fields and the stubble turned over as ploughing commences in preparation for autumn sowing.

By September the orchard trees are laden with apples and plums, assuming the wasps have spared them. Huge dragonflies still manoeuvre swiftly over the water and around the garden, their frequent prey, butterflies, are still in evidence and red admirals in particular are attracted to the ripening fruit in the orchards. The songbirds are quiet or absent. Moulting has already taken place, the finches have spread out over the surrounding arable fields and hedgerows, and the summer migrants which we so welcomed in March and April have left or are shortly to leave for warmer climes.

Fungus appears as if by magic. 'Fairy rings' on the lawn and mushrooms and puffballs in the fields tell me that autumn is here, to say nothing of some fairly exotic growths on the old apple trees.

A man used to ride by on his bicycle every autumn collecting mushrooms. He would come past the house every other day for some weeks, had a basket on the handlebars and always wore a flat cap.

The basket contained the mushrooms, or to be more specific, 'blueys' as he called them. He was I think retired and spent most of his time at this season of the year searching all the fields round about, and evidently selling the mushrooms in order to provide some income.

He justified his presence to me, thinking no doubt that I might be a little suspicious, with the words 'No need to worry about me. I'm all right, I am. They all know me around here'. A figure from a bygone age I always felt, living off the land, but I haven't seen him for some years.

The nut trees by the orchard are clustered with hazel nuts, or filberts, presently in green casings or sheaths which later release the brown nuts so sought after by squirrels and jays. The grey squirrels can be seen burying the nuts to provide a larder for the winter. They will dig them up again later but those which are not found may sprout in the following year to provide new saplings and more nut trees.

The leaves on many trees are now beginning to change colour, a sign of the autumn fall to come. The chestnuts are among the first, and the oak, ash, maple and hawthorns soon follow. There are red berries on the thorn hedges and on the hollies, and the yew trees are festooned with sticky fruit. A bounty for the birds and squirrels as winter sets in.

Ducks gather again on the river above the mill race, the moorhens become less territorial and egrets visit the margins more frequently. Herons come to fish in the evenings looking huge as they glide down in the gloaming to their favourite spot, and kingfishers still `zoom` up and down stream. On warm evenings bats quarter the twilight air in their endless search for moths and other flying insects.

September is the time of the local ploughing match which moves between a number of venues from year to year and, I have noticed, is more often than not accompanied by glorious weather.

One year the chosen site was a field adjacent to my land and very close to the house. The spectacle was amazing and what a contrast! There were hundreds of people, horses, farm implements, tents, dog shows, caterers and a licensed bar! That was a potential bonus, a 'pub' within a few yards of the house, even if only for a day. In truth I didn't really take advantage of this particular opportunity but Roger, my neighbouring farmer and show organiser that year, did present me with a bottle of malt whisky afterwards, to compensate me for any inconvenience!

In October the hunting scene makes its presence felt, and the hounds are sometimes exercised on the bridleway, always accompanied by one of the kennel staff on a bicycle. I confess I am no enthusiast for the sport of fox hunting but there is something very traditional and essentially rural about the sight of hounds being exercised on an autumn morning.

When the hunt 'in full cry' attempted to cross my land on one occasion, the hounds stampeded through my garden, crossed the river and headed upstream, frightening the water birds and the sheep as they went, to say nothing of any small children who might have been around at the time. This was a little unnerving I must admit.

Autumn creates its own special atmosphere, marked by falling leaves, a crispness in the air, the low angle of the sun and the lengthening of the shadows. The unmistakeable scent of damp earth and rotting leaves and in particular, bonfire smoke all add to the ambience.

There is nothing so characteristic of the closing months of the year than the smell of a bonfire, particularly when it is burning leaves. One of my greatest pleasures on a cold day is to light a good fire in the orchard and watch the smoke curling round in the breeze whilst enjoying the heat from the flames.

When lit late in the afternoon, the smoke merges with the mist as dusk approaches, and if I can keep the flames crackling and the shadows leaping I am in my element! Simple pleasures I know, which date back to the beginning of mankind, but there's nothing wrong with that. And the smell of that smoke. Somebody should bottle it!

Winters in these parts are not what they used to be, but gales still blow any remaining leaves off the trees in November and December, the rains seem to just keep coming, the river level rises, the days get shorter and the nights blacker. The sheep have gone for the winter as the grass will no longer sustain them, and the ewes need to meet up with the ram in order to start the whole process off again.

The winter thrushes return to feed on the berries which cover the hedgerows, the robin sings plaintively and sometimes a song thrush if the weather is mild, but otherwise the countryside is quiet.

The squirrels are busy however and a big mistle thrush is in charge of the yew trees, guarding their sticky berries against all comers for as long as it can. Stoats still look for mice and rabbits, and owls hunt through the long nights.

Siskins and redpolls, those little finches from northern lands, haunt the tops of the alder trees by the water, and the occasional woodcock is flushed from the ground cover when I go exploring in hard weather. Snipe used to feed at the river edges where the mud stays soft but I rarely see them now.

In December and January dog foxes bark and vixens scream on freezing nights, their cries carrying far across the bleak landscape and although I have heard them many times, the sound still makes me shiver.

Snow is infrequent and does not often lie for long, but many years ago I was marooned once or twice when drifts three feet deep or more covered much of the drive to the house. I tried shovelling the snow to clear a way for my car but got nowhere and had to be rescued by Derek, the agricultural contractor from the village who made a path through with his tractor.

In the meantime, I had little option but to give up the idea of going to the office, and instead lit a log fire and enjoyed the isolation. Much better to be snowed in than snowed out I decided, having more than once had to abandon my car by the road in the middle of the night and struggle through deep drifts, on one occasion wearing black tie and a dinner suit, in order to reach the shelter of the house. Alone at night in a near arctic landscape with not a living soul to be seen or heard, a total 'white out' as far as the eye could see and wearing evening garb was quite an experience.

The absolute silence of the snowy landscape seemed to engulf me, the only sound being the crunch of my highly unsuitable shoes in the snow as I walked the quarter mile to the house, my footprints the only witness to the episode, apart that is from my abandoned car! The sky was truly dark and the cold intense.

These were exceptional times for this part of the country however and who knows if and when we may see them again. Most winters seem to be mild and wet nowadays but every year we know that Christmas will come and go, the winter jasmine will glow brightly on the front of the house and in due course the snowdrops and aconites will emerge again to herald a new beginning.

A Page from the Diary

Quiet, brightish start.   Heron on bank behind mill, Egret in river below bridge (am)   Lovely sunny, fresh day, later.   Buzzard 'mewing' loudly from fields near the drive (am), Barn Owl hunting at noon over 'ha ha' field. Watched it for some time gliding, twisting, hovering often within a few yards of me, incredible views. Pounced into the grass several times but not sure whether caught anything.   Moorhen on the water with solitary chick.   Jays noisily scolding something, or each other, in plantation, like 'tearing linen'!   Buzzard soaring over nearby village(pm), mobbed by Sparrow Hawk?   Butterflies about and Damsel and Dragonflies, Red Admiral and small Tortoiseshell on buddleja.   Later (pm) two Buzzards overhead, soaring together...

Jays 'scolding' again towards plantation.

A Page from the Diary

August 29th 2007

Bright periods and showers, some thunder.   *Kingfisher under*

bridge and flying downstream, Moorhens busy as usual, again hostile

to young bird from their own brood!   *Heron flying over close to*

house, geese (feral Greylags) also passing over, Dragonflies everywhere.

Dusk 8.30 pm…Barn Owls and Geese!   *What a show!*   *Two*

Barn Owls flying together around barn field area. Much 'snoring' from

nesting barn!   *Later young owl flew straight from barn towards me*

and came within three/four yards before turning away, and repeated

behaviour a number of times before finally going back to barns.   *I*

am sure it mistook me (with white hair) for an owl on a post in the

fading light.   *Two foxes crossed the field, one behind the other,*

Rabbits watching them.   *Bats flying around and a crescent (quarter)*

moon bright in the sky to the west.   *Heron gliding over low.*   *Then*

the geese came, skein after skein, small and large groups, came so low

you could hear the wind in their pinions as they passed overhead.

CHAPTER VII

The Water Mill

According to local archives, milling here has been documented back as far as 1086, and during the 1500's at least, the mill standing at that time was owned by a nearby monastery or priory.

The present structure although built on an ancient site was erected in 1778, of brick and pantile construction, and incorporates a 14 ft diameter undershot wooden water wheel. There are three floors including a loft from where the grain sacks were emptied into chutes which gravity fed three pairs of circular millstones.

Storage and work areas make up the ground floor space, including a workshop with fireplace and a huge cog or gearwheel which drives the stones and the grain hoist directly from the water wheel. Interestingly I am informed that the many gears and cogs which power the stones are largely made of apple wood, being less likely to spark and cause fire than other materials.

A piece of industrial history much appreciated by local archaeological society members who used to request visits to view and tour the building and its workings from time to time. Strangely they don't come anymore. Probably because I told them that the floors were partly rotten and I wasn't insured if any one dropped through. A shame really as on occasions they had been known to give me a bottle of wine or something stronger for my trouble!

An organisation specialising in the supply and installation of turbines for the generation of electricity approached me one time, and later came to do a survey of the existing mill wheel and waterway. I got quite excited about the prospect of getting free power from the river but at the end of the day my hopes were dashed when their report said that due to the comparative lack of height of the fall and the average flow rate, I could at best only hope to achieve enough current to power a couple of table lamps! Ah well, at least I found out and saved the very considerable cost of a turbine.

Ironically the man who came to do the survey and who had travelled a long way couldn't start his car afterwards. Fortunately, I had a set of jump leads in my garage and was able to get him going, otherwise he might have been with me for the weekend!

Fairly early in my time here it became necessary to carry out repairs to one of the walls between the mill and the house. This wall is adjacent to the main sluice and supports the massive timber shaft which carries the mill wheel. It is also partly under water and in order to gain access to the damaged brickwork Cyd, my builder friend, had to dam the water upstream and divert the flow into the bypass channel.

It took a week or so before the river could be returned to its normal course and during this period the house was strangely quiet. Because the effect of the rushing water is normally constant I am not always conscious of it, but I certainly missed the sound during those few days when it was diverted. The silence was something I just wasn't used to!

The temperature inside the mill is peculiarly cold, even on a warm summer day, and the water roars past, although no longer driving the wheel. The mill sleeps, having not been used for over fifty years and is now inhabited by Jackdaws.

Every year a pair of stock doves build their flimsy nest under the roof tiles of the 'lean to' cart shed which is attached to the mill and I listen to their familiar 'woo wup' calls in the mornings. A similar size to the more familiar wood pigeon, this dove is distinguished from the former by the lack of a white 'ring' around its neck, and is much less numerous

And then there were the rats. Shortly after I took possession of the property I noticed that there were rats coming down in droves from the mill, seemingly to drink from the water's edge. I had never seen so many rats in one place and seriously thought to send for the 'Pied Piper'! They were living on the remains of the spilt grain which was abundant amongst the mill machinery and storage rooms but I am glad to say they left after a time when the food evidently ran out. Good riddance to them. I am not so comfortable with too many rats about.

Having said that there are still odd rats to be seen, especially in the winter months. They come to eat fallen apples in the orchard, but one year a rat tried to eat its way through my back door.

Of particular note was 'Grandfather Rat', an ancient member of its tribe which appeared regularly for a time on the back yard wall following a route from the mill to the river banks. This animal shuffled along, rather than ran, it's fur was dishevelled and lank, it had a long scaly tail and pink feet and was very large by rat standards.

It emerged every evening following the same path and at the same time. I have noticed this about rats before. You can almost set your watch by their appearance and they invariably stick to well established ways or 'runs'.

One day it confronted a jackdaw on the grassy bank and there was something of a 'stand off'. I wondered what would happen but after taking a somewhat threatening stance both rat and jackdaw backed away. I am not at all sure the rat was up to any kind of contest anyway and the jackdaw seemed to sense this.

Soon after this incident I found the rat's corpse in the coal house where it had evidently died of old age. Maybe it was the one which attempted to eat a way through my door? I should be safe now!

On another occasion a troop of rats appeared to be eating the moss in my lawn night after night during very hard frosty weather. This was after dark and I shone a torch from my window one evening to see what they were up to. The torch beam picked out at least eight pairs of close set red eyes!

But enough of these inevitable denizens of the riverside. When looking at the mill which was one of six on a stretch of water only a few miles long it is convenient to consider the waterway itself. A slow flowing lowland river or beck beloved of moorhens and mallard, it meets after a couple more miles, and another mill, the river Trent.

The water only becomes a torrent when it reaches the mill race and the abrupt fall of the overflow or bypass, but it nevertheless attracts grey wagtails, very much a hill stream bird, and on one remarkable day a dipper or water ouzel, a member of the thrush family which hunts under the surface of fast flowing water. Fish of various kinds haunt the depths and I have seen trout, perch and pike but most of the fish I believe are chubb.

There is however a deep and undisturbed stretch much shaded by overhanging trees and undergrowth, where in hot weather in summer quite large fish rise up and break the surface before rolling over, showing silvery sides before submerging. I think these may be bream but I confess I am by no means certain, and I never see them at any other time of the year, probably because they go back to their deep water habitat.

The first trout I ever tasted was caught in this water, when my uncle brought a fair sized fish to our family home one morning when I was a child. He had caught it about a mile upstream from here and we had it for breakfast.

A bridleway crosses the land, and the river by a ford and a bridge. The ford provides a regular drinking place for small birds, and robins, goldfinches, yellow buntings, blackbirds and others take full advantage. Some of the horses and riders enjoy splashing through the water but others are very nervous and 'skittish' at the prospect. On one occasion a rider was thrown and the horse demolished a nearby gate but fortunately there was no serious injury incurred.

A group of artists one day asked if they could set up their easels on the bridge with a view to painting the view of the water and the mill. I was pleased that they asked permission and hoped they had a nice day but I never saw any results of their labours, nor have I heard from them since. Many passing walkers take photographs and there must be hundreds if not thousands of these in circulation. But I suppose it's not such a price to pay for living in a picturesque location.

I have a small rowing boat and spent many happy hours taking my niece Natasha and nephews Alex and Nicholas up the river when they were small. There were a few near misses when the boat almost capsized due to overcrowding but generally this pastime was a great success and enjoyed by all.

It is noticeable how one gets a different perspective when seeing very familiar surroundings from the water, whether wading or in a boat. It all had a touch of Enid Blyton, especially when we picnicked on the banks.

Being an ancient site and at the junction of three parishes it seems likely that the hedge which borders the drive could be very old, particularly as with the accompanying ditch it forms the boundary or meeting point of two of these districts.

This theory is borne out I think by the number of tree species which make up the hedge. Over its quarter mile length there are maple, hawthorn, blackthorn, elder, oak, ash, hazel, holly, honeysuckle, hops, wild rose, bramble and ivy.

Another suggestion as to the hedge's status may be found in ancient records which refer in 1574 to a `a hedge, 'extending in length by the said hedge to a mill' standing on the beck. Could it be the same hedge, as it is mentioned in connection with a 'boundary of the manor'?

Behind the house and adjacent to the ha ha is a field, bordered by the river, which once supported withy beds. These were shallow trench like features designed for the commercial growth of willows, which when young produce supple willow stems or wands used for weaving in to baskets, wicker furniture and fencing.

There is no sign of this activity now, at least from ground level, but I was informed by someone from the local university some years ago that the original beds or trenches can still be identified from the air.

This was a complete surprise to me, and I have not been up to look, but shortly after this time a number of students spent some days examining the site and making digs in order to confirm the findings.

Resulting from this investigation I am now prohibited from doing anything to change the landscape of the field or even planting trees on it.

One evening I received a phone call from someone I did not know, who claimed to have been allowed by Wilf to fish for eels just upstream from the mill race. He asked me if I would grant him permission to continue this activity but I declined his request. I had never seen an eel in the river and have never seen one since! I suspect he was after trout.

The water provides constant interest and at times drama. Heavy or prolonged rainstorms cause it to flow in 'spate' creating huge volumes which thunder past my kitchen and reach levels considerably higher than the floors of the house. The resulting surge is held back by a wide and very substantial wall alongside the back yard, but only this prevents the water from pouring right through the house.

There can be a problem though when tree branches, logs and other debris carried down by high water can jam in the sluice after heavy and persistent rain. I have, more times than I care to remember, had to clear the sluice late at night, balancing on a slippery beam over the flow and dragging the 'log jam' piece by piece out of the water. With no one to help, this task is quite risky as one slip in the darkness and nobody within half a mile or so to assist, would have put me in some trouble. Fortunately, these incidents, apart from being a bit too dramatic at times, and giving me something of a wetting, have not so far caused me any harm.

I remember one Christmas morning when after much heavy rain during what turned out to be an exceptionally wet night I got up to find the sluice jammed with debris. It so happened that I had been invited by my friends Geoff and Marjory for a Christmas breakfast but instead of enjoying their hospitality I had first to clear the sluice. Whilst they and most other sane people therefore were enjoying the delights of a festive morning I was risking life and limb, balancing on a beam only inches above a raging torrent, struggling in the cold and wet to prevent a possible flood.

When I eventually arrived very late for the breakfast after a good wash and change of clothes to find everyone drinking champagne and enjoying croissants, muffins and 'pigs in blankets', they all thought my story was hilarious, and I received little sympathy for my plight. What a start to Christmas. You couldn't make it up!

Once the best part of a whole garden shed came down on the flood. This was ridiculous. At times like this George Eliot's famous novel `The Mill on the Floss` comes to mind and it is always a relief when the level starts to go down, even though neither I, nor Wilf before me, have ever seen water in the house during eighty years of occupation.

Fortunately, the incidents of driftwood and other debris causing difficulties with the sluice are now much reduced. Some years back I had a `stickle` put in upstream. This is a series of posts hammered in across the river bed and protruding above the surface of the water to catch any large objects which may be floating down.

Occasionally when the water is very high it spills over the banks upstream and partially floods the ha ha field, forming a shallow lake. This attracts even more ducks, gulls and often wading birds and can be quite a spectacle when viewed from the house.

After an unusually long period of heavy rain the nearby gravel pit lake flooded one time, the water engulfing the lower part of my drive and effectively cutting me off, except by four-wheel drive! Flooding of this kind is nothing however when compared with that suffered from time to time by residents in some of the local villages, who have had to contend with water in their homes, and access by boat when the river Trent bursts its banks. Fortunately, floods of this kind do not occur often these days, but I remember a time when they were not so unusual.

There are discarded circular mill stones around the back yard and in the floor of a building which I use as a coal house, and which also contains an ancient bread oven and a copper. These features are built in to the brick work and I think of similar age to the mill.

Water was pumped from the river to another building next to the coal house which I understand was known as the 'cheese house'. Someone must have made cheeses here at one time, and hand operated lead pumps were still installed when I arrived, together with a large underground tank to store water. The tank we filled in as I did not fancy water underneath the floor, and the building joined to the house to form what is now a dining room.

Something else I have had to tackle is the question of invasive plant life affecting the flow and the banks. In the early years the stretch of water above the mill became choked with reeds in the summer months and I spent hours wading in the water, which was often nearly up to my waist, naively trying to pull the reeds out by the roots and throwing them onto the bank to try to prevent them from growing again.

This was hot and tiring work and not so effective but I persisted for several seasons before being informed that they could be sprayed with a chemical which would not harm the fish. I now have this done every couple of years or so and the water flows freely but I wouldn't mind having the hours back that I wasted on such a thankless task!

Other water plants present no real problem, although rafts of water cress can become too prolific at times. One day however Joyce, the local post lady who used to come all the way up the long drive on her bicycle in all weathers to deliver my mail, told me that she had recently been on holiday in the lake district and whilst there, had noticed some spectacular pink flowering plants growing by water.

It then transpired that she had brought some back for me, thinking that they would look really nice growing at the side of the beck. This was a kind gesture and I duly planted them, fortunately down stream, but then didn't give them any more thought.

Little did I know what a nightmare they would become, for they proved to be Himalayan balsam, a waterside plant that grows to be enormous and spreads like wildfire. Many of the stems grow to nearly three inches thick at the base and up to five or six feet tall. They are a menace in spite of their colourful flowers and I have been trying to get rid of them ever since.

In the early 1980's during an exceptionally cold winter the river froze right across and the ice was so thick I could have walked or ridden a bicycle down the middle. It was like a pavement and the water fall at the mill race formed giant icicles. I remember a coot and a dabchick appeared and stayed for several days where the area under the foot bridge remained free of ice.

In fine weather the sheer beauty of the sunlight shimmering on the wavelets as the water rushes by, and the ever present sound from the tumbling fall at the mill race fill my senses. In the summer months, bright blue damsel flies hover over the surface and broods of tiny black moorhen chicks and little ducklings scud about exploring their watery world and snapping up flying insects.

It is noticeable that although moorhens feed their chicks for some time when they are very small, ducklings fend for themselves from the moment they hit the water, the mother duck making no attempt to provide food.

On clear nights the moon makes its presence felt, reflecting in the water and creating an ever moving silvery trail to lighten the darkness.

The water is a constant source of interest and forms a running backdrop to everything I do. Ever changing in mood from lazy flow to raging torrent but always there, running free as it has for generations and will for long after I am gone.

The mill watches on, silent and at rest.

A Page from the Diary

June 7th 2008

Wet in night, drizzle this morning. *Kestrel visiting nest box and female inside, so nest is ok after all.* *Kept very low profile since eggs laid.* *So Barn Owls and Kestrels nesting within about ten feet of each other (through walls).* *Later visits more regular... eggs must have hatched?* *Goldcrests singing in garden(pm), plus Blackbirds, Chiffchaff, Willow Warbler etc.... beautiful!* *Poppies in rape field by drive look great, Buzzard overhead mobbed by Carrion Crow, Redshank calling.* *Very summery afternoon...warm!* *8-9pm Barn Owl came in with prey four times within 40 minutes, always hunting in same direction... flying away swiftly and coming back gliding at considerable height, holding prey (voles I think) in left foot and 'power diving' (like a falcon) down to aperture in barn with unerring accuracy. Cock Blackbird singing on another barn roof about 25ft away completely unconcerned!*

A Page from the Diary

Beautiful sunny morning, blue skies and warm in the sun. Buzzard

glided over (am), Brimstone butterflies about. Jackdaws and

Magpies nest building, Song Thrush singing, Violets and Cellandines

in bloom. Hawthorn leaves just starting to show in sheltered spots.

Mallard drakes on the water. Green Woodpeckers 'yaffling',

Buzzard low over 'ha ha' field (pm). Small Tortoiseshell butterfly

in yard garden. Think the winter thrushes have left us? Later...I

was too hasty, heard Fieldfares 'chattering' in the orchard (pm).

Two pairs of Teal on water behind mill, late afternoon. Delightfully

neat and smart little ducks in full breeding plumage.

CHAPTER VIII

Uninvited Guests

Possibly the most extraordinary thing to happen to me in all my time here, is quite simply all about a robin. I remember the incident in every detail, almost as though it occurred only yesterday.

In fact thirty years or more have intervened since I was woken one summer morning at about five am by the song of a robin. But this was no ordinary awakening, the bird was in my bedroom and sounded extremely loud! This was unsurprising as the robin was singing whilst perched on the brass rail at the end of my bed.

It is usual for me to sleep with a window partially open but a bird which found itself on the inside, would in almost any circumstances, flutter about trying to get out. This robin perched on the end of the bed and sang like a living alarm clock!

Lying half awake briefly wondering what to do about it I noticed what appeared to be smoke drifting through the bedroom door which was slightly open. On jumping out of bed to investigate I went on to the landing and found the air thick with smoke. I rushed down to the kitchen and found towels already alight hanging on the front of the Aga, and the rush matting, which at that time covered the floor, was in flames where it butted up to the cooker.

I had no difficulty putting out the fire and opened all the windows to let out the smoke, whilst at the same time thanking my lucky stars that things were no worse. The walls and curtains were smoke damaged and there would have to be cleaning and some redecoration, but it was a beautiful new day and I was unharmed!

A lucky escape, but was it more than that? Was it a coincidence that the robin came into my bedroom and sang so loudly at the precise moment that the house was filling with smoke and could have gone up in flames? The odds must be millions to one against. Or was the bird part of some divine intervention to save my life?

I will never know for sure, but have often thought that things sometimes happen in life which we are simply not meant to understand. May be this was one of those, but it would take a very persuasive argument to convince me that the visit from this robin was somehow all down to chance.

Other visitors over the years have included a little owl, and several swallows which must have come down a bedroom chimney, blue tits, wrens, very large bumble bees and hibernating queen wasps. However, for entertainment value, or eccentricity, depending on how you view such episodes there have also been several night time incidents with bats.

I have been woken in the middle of the night more than once by the whirring flight of a bat circling my room at high speed. On some circuits the bat actually passed underneath the bed! I could of course have left matters to sort themselves out either by the creature finding its own way out or going to roost hanging on the curtains. But no, I had to go downstairs to find a child's fishing net which I had kept from when my niece and nephews were small, and stand on the bed in just my pyjamas trying to catch the bat as it circled the room.

Not only did this feel like the actions of a crazy man but I can confirm that trying to intercept the swift passage of a bat with its swoops, twists and turns in a confined space is not as easy as it might sound. And all this at something like two o'clock in the morning!

My fairly acrobatic attempts did on each occasion meet with success in the end and I was able to free the little `flying mouse` from the net and allow it to fly off into the night to continue its hunting, but I was always pleased on these occasions that I had no neighbours to observe my antics.

Sometimes, even in daylight, bats have flown in to the kitchen and travelled from room to room before I have been able to catch them... again with that invaluable child's fishing net!

More serious was an invasion of stoats which decided to set up home in the small loft over the dining room, which I had converted from the original cheese house. I knew there would be trouble when I first noticed the regular passage of these handsome but ruthless little predators running along the guttering outside the kitchen window.

About a foot long, chestnut coloured with white underparts and a black tip to the tail, the most disturbing thing about these animals is that they appear to show little or no fear of humans. They stare straight at you in almost a dismissive way and are not too inclined to give ground.

They looked at me through the kitchen window completely unfazed as if daring me to interfere. I hoped at first they were just hunting in and out of the roof tiles but by their repeated visits it was soon evident that they were here to stay.

I could hear them from inside, running over the rafters and when I opened the access trap door to the loft, having first made sure they were out, it became obvious from the smell that they were bringing in prey and probably had young. This was too much, even for me with my keen interest in nature. Why couldn't they bring up their family in the adjacent mill? This would have been perfect and there must be plenty of mice in there to provide them with food.

My answer was to call in a pest control officer from the local council but he didn't fancy a confrontation with angry stoats and wouldn't enter the loft. I would have to find another way to persuade them to leave.

I was fairly sure I had heard somewhere that squirrels could be dissuaded by loud noise and I thought that if it worked for squirrels it would very probably work for stoats.

So I waited until I could hear their footsteps on the ceiling and then I opened the trap door, having taken a brass tray and an old soup spoon with me, put my head and shoulders through the opening and banged the spoon on the tray continuously as though I were ringing a gong. It made a terrible noise and I repeated the process a number of times over a few days, in fact whenever I heard them scampering across the ceiling.

To my relief they eventually left for a more peaceful hideaway, but this was not quite the end of my problem.

After a day or two I began to notice an unusual number of large flies, meat flies my mother used to call them, in the kitchen and in the room under the loft. This was alarming. On getting home from my `day job` in the early evening I was having to kill or expel somewhere around thirty large black flies from the kitchen before I could even think about preparing something to eat. There was also an unpleasant smell and I began to realise that the flies and the smell were coming from the remains of animal prey which the stoats had been bringing in for their young and which remained in the loft.

I discovered that the flies were coming in to the house through a crack in the plaster by one of the beams in the ceiling and I am glad to say this proved to be their only access, for after stopping this up the flies ceased to worry me and the smell gradually subsided.

What a relief! Stoats are always welcome outside where they belong, and where they play their part in the delicate balance of nature, but I do not want them in my roof!

Neither do I appreciate hornets or mice, but living in the country one has to compromise sometimes. Huge hornets moved in under the tiled roof just above my bedroom one year. Occasionally they got in the house and they were so large that when flying outside after dark they even made the security lights come on. Seems that unlike wasps they also fly at night. Furthermore, I am not at all sure about the severity of their stings, and do not really want to find out!

Masonry bees search for cracks in the mortar between the brickwork of the house, and the cottage, on warm sunny days, and even try to find homes in the keyholes of the doors. But they are harmless, as far as I know, and rarely find their way inside.

Jackdaws seem obsessed with trying to nest in my chimneys, so much so that I have had to wire all the chimney pots to prevent their access. A pair nest in the mill chimney which is fine, but if I let them have their way with the house I wouldn't be able to use a single fireplace. Jackdaws almost seem to prefer chimneys to more natural cavities when it comes to nest building, yet the chimneys hardly appear ideal to us, being vertical shafts in which it must be difficult to secure a nest, to say nothing of being full of soot.

But I suppose if you were born in a chimney you might well go back to one, in spite of any problems it might present!

Whilst on the subject of chimneys, a sweep who used to come here was a real character. He was fairly short and rounded in stature, with a ruddy complexion and wore a black beret. He was very amiable and looked like a sweep, but when he put his brushes up the chimney he used to sit on the floor by the hearth singing at the top of his voice.

He must have been happy in his work but didn't seem to remove too much soot. I am sure Mary Poppins would have approved though!

I have set traps and caught many mice in the loft but unfortunately not before they had bitten through some electricity cables and put my lights out!

Another problem was caused by the appearance of two tiny black water shrews which came in one morning via an open bathroom window. I managed to catch one of them in a glass jar as it ran around on the floor and return it to the outdoors, but it's companion disappeared somehow into the structure of the house.

A few days later I became aware of a most unpleasant smell from the water in the taps, somewhat reminiscent of a dead body! This was not good news and on examination of the water supply tank in the loft space the shrew, or rather the remains of it were found by the plumber floating in the water.

The animal must have been attracted by the presence of a large volume of water in the tank and found it's way up to the loft where it subsequently died, thereby contaminating my supply.

Toads appear on or around the front doorstep on summer nights and they are very welcome, but I sometimes have to persuade them not to enter the house.

Unusual circumstances applied to another visitor which turned out to be rather permanent! Ian who lived in the village downstream regularly walked the mile or so to the farm at weekends, always accompanied by his dog, and we became good friends, often putting the world to rights over a coffee on Sunday mornings.

Several years passed before one day Ian phoned to say his dog had unfortunately died, and he asked if she could be buried in my garden. The reasoning behind this request was that the dog so enjoyed the weekend walks over such a long period that his owner thought that my grounds would be a fitting place to lay her to rest.

How could I say no? I agreed that so long as he performed the burial I would be happy for the dog to be interred in a corner of the orchard where the snowdrops grow. For some time afterwards Ian visited the site on a regular basis to pay his respects and I feel sure he must have taken some comfort from the fact that she was amongst the snowdrops.

In the garden I am a little ashamed to admit, I did at one time engage in something of a war with moles. When their 'hills' started to appear in the lawn and surrounding areas I panicked a bit and commenced to set traps. These were spring loaded 'pincers' which have to be set below ground in the moles' runs.

Admittedly, success was very limited and I did not like the idea of killing them in this way, so I tried smoke bombs which are placed in the run and ignited, the resulting smoke being intended to drive the creatures away. This did not seem to work either as the 'bombs' became extinguished due to a lack of sufficient air.

I gave up in the end and left the moles alone. Oddly I don't seem to be bothered with them now. Although they dig around in the surrounding fields and in the orchard, evidence of their subterranean activities in my garden is now rare.

My ongoing battle with rabbits is another matter, but this is purely defensive. Rabbits in the garden were at one time a disaster. They ate everything and dug holes in all the wrong places ! I had to wire the whole area before I could create anything which could call itself a garden, and even then the occasional rabbit breaches my defences by swimming across the river!

Outside the garden they are not too much of a problem except that they de-bark and consequently kill young trees unless they are protected, and constantly dig holes along the edges of the drive. The baby ones are admittedly cute, so small you could put them in a tea cup, but they grow bigger!

There are far too many, but disease reduces their ranks every so often and they do provide a meal for the stoats and foxes, as well as buzzards on occasion.

Grey squirrels I also have to live with. They bite off the berries and many of the stems from the holly bushes at the beginning of winter, so I never have any for Christmas! They sever much of the new growth from the yews at times, leaving a carpet of small branches and shoots on the ground. They raid the bird table and sometimes the feeders which are intended for small birds and they predate eggs and young birds from nests in the spring.

Like magpies and rabbits there are just too many, and they do, at least locally, upset the balance of nature but they were here before I came, and will I am sure, be here long after I have gone.

All part of life 'at the mill' I suppose, and I have to take visitors in my stride, whether they be saviours or pests. It's just that some of them seem to want to live rather too close to me!

A Page from the Diary

July 18th 2010

Kingfisher on sheep hurdle again, family of well grown ducklings on water, plus Moorhens including one tiny chick... are there any more? Red Admiral, Tortoiseshell and Comma butterflies around buddleia. Also smaller grey brown ones (not sure of these)... but no Painted Ladies this year. Large Dragonfly on the wing. Kingfisher on bank behind mill fishing (pm), then noticed it had turned its beak upward at about 30 degrees. Wondered why until after probably 30 seconds or so a Hobby came in to view, sailing high overhead! Eventually moved away and Kingfisher resumed its task! Many bees on the lavender flowers, Goldfinches constantly twittering and singing from the tree tops.

A Page from the Diary

May 29th 2011

Dullish, windy, light showers but no real rain.   Goldfinches around garden, Swallows and House Martins 'hawking' low over wild flower meadows.   Pair of Moorhens with one chick in front of mill 'saw off' a Grey Squirrel which came too close to the water's edge.   Mallard drakes on water and resting behind mill.   Cool. Windy eve, but saw Barn Owl in orchard, Hobby overhead, two Mute Swans flying, a Fox cub on drive, heard Green Woodpecker, Song thrush, Blackcap and Blackbird singing, plus Goldfinches and Chaffinch.   Swifts overhead and Swallows lower down around orchard (eve).

CHAPTER IX

Prey and Predators

One thing which quickly becomes apparent when living so close to the natural world is that most wild creatures are either predator or prey, and more often than not, both. From small insects to some of the largest animals to roam the planet this rule applies, and we humans also play our part.

This is not the plains of Africa, far from it, but when observing the behaviour of animals in the wild, even here in the UK, it is possible to witness some dramatic scenes which, albeit on a much smaller scale, are not so different to something you might see in the Serengeti.

In a previous chapter I have described the incident involving a Heron's attempts to swallow a rat, which was spectacular enough, and the sparrow hawk which appeared to be trying to drown a starling, both observed from my kitchen window, but just when I think I have seen it all I come across further examples of unusual or even extreme behaviour, which surprise and in some cases genuinely shock me.

In most years a pair of mistle thrushes build their nest in one of the orchard trees, or within one of the nearby plantations. Never once however in all the years I have lived here have the birds been successful in raising a brood.

This thrush is a favourite of mine due to its bold nature and its habit of singing from the tree tops in early spring, often in stormy weather, hence the sometimes used country name of 'stormcock'. It is an early nester and favouring elevated sites, often in the forks of trees before they come into leaf, the nest is an easy target for crows and magpies which steal their eggs or young.

In spite of the thrush`s rather depressing lack of success to date, I was more optimistic one year when the birds chose a high fork in an old apple tree close to the garden where I could keep an eye on it. The nest was duly built and the blossom and the leaves were starting to emerge as the thrush commenced to brood, while her mate did his best to noisily scold and harass any potential intruder.

The mistle thrush is habitually a brave and determined defender of its nest site and will even attack humans on occasions. I have been `dive bombed` by them and the experience is off putting to say the least, but this threatening behaviour is not always enough to see off a determined predator.

One day on hearing the bird's alarm calls I approached the tree just as a magpie arrived and flew straight to the nest. There ensued a terrible commotion as the thrushes attempted to defend their home and after thirty seconds or so the magpie and one of the thrushes tumbled from the tree apparently locked together in combat.

They fell to the ground a few yards away in long grass and nettles, the thrush screaming, and when I ran over to investigate or even try to prevent the likely outcome the magpie flew away leaving the dying thrush on the ground, its head almost severed from its body.

This was murder, or at least that was my, to be fair, too hasty a reaction! I cannot recall a similar case, where a magpie has literally dragged a sitting bird off its nest and killed it in this way, though they will steal the eggs or young from undefended nests. This was a sad and ironic consequence of the fearless stance taken by the parent birds, but the magpie should not be blamed for striving to find food for its own family.

The 'boss man' of the resident birds around here however is the carrion crow, the dominant member of its tribe, second only to the much larger and comparatively rare raven. The carrion crow will mob and chase off any bird, even those much larger than itself, if it considers them a threat to its territory, and in particular its nest site.

Any buzzard or heron which dares to fly in to its `air space' suffers an attack and is angrily pursued until well out of range, especially during the spring months. I have seen kestrels and even sparrow hawks mobbed, although I did once witness a large female sparrow hawk turn the tables and pursue its attacker at low altitude for some distance, the crow twisting and turning in the air before eventually making its escape. This was however a dangerous game and on another day the crow could have been killed.

In fairness it should be pointed out that the crow is itself a significant predator and a notorious robber of eggs and nestlings in the springtime.

There are many pairs of the crow's smaller cousins, the jackdaws, nesting in the mill, occupying spaces in the chimney, the loft and in nest boxes originally installed to attract barn owls.

I love to have these birds around. Although having much in common with other members of the crow family, only the rook shares its gregarious nature and habit of nesting close together whenever circumstances allow.

They are very vocal, their constant 'jack' or 'chack a chack' calls cheer me and I am frequently entertained by their antics as they race and chase each other through the air. The Jackdaw is I think one of the comparatively few birds which appears to fly for fun.

The carrion crow is mobbed and 'dive bombed' by the jackdaws whenever it flies or perches anywhere near the mill during the breeding season. Having observed this behaviour many times I am convinced that the crow invites the attention by deliberately straying in to the jackdaw's space just to upset them. The crow is clearly regarded as a threat but in truth I feel sure it is just being mischievous. These 'games' are enacted out every morning during the early part of the year and I reckon both crow and jackdaws thoroughly enjoy the contest.

In other circumstances the carrion crow can be a considerable adversary. One morning I was working in the garden when I became aware of a noisy commotion from under the weeping ash tree by the ha ha. On investigation it transpired that this time a magpie was the victim of a determined attack by a crow, which seemed to be pinning the smaller bird to the ground and using its strong beak to pummel it into submission.

Now here again was something I have never witnessed before and which must be highly unusual. A crow attacking and killing a young bird or a small or weakened animal is one thing, but taking on a comparatively strong and wily bird like a magpie, a fellow member of the crow family, was very surprising. Both birds flew away when disturbed however so maybe there was not too much harm done.

I have seen foxes catching rabbits, and kestrels and owls hunting mice and voles but the most formidable and efficient hunter around these parts is my old friend the stoat. I would guess this animal enjoys a higher success rate than even the big cats on the African savannahs. Once it locks onto its prey, often a rabbit, there is little hope for its intended victim.

One frosty winter's day when out walking, I saw a rabbit running through the orchard, followed at about twenty yards by a stoat. This was fascinating and I stayed to watch, to see what the outcome would be.

The rabbit seemed aware that it was being tracked by the stoat and kept running but sometimes pausing, almost as though encouraging the stoat to catch up. The stoat followed every twist and turn but did not seem to be in any hurry. Eventually the rabbit left cover and plotted a course across the short grass of an open field, followed every step of the way by the stoat which then began to speed up.

After a while the rabbit just seemed to give up and froze almost as though awaiting its fate. The stoat quickly went in for the kill but the rabbit did not die immediately so there followed a bit of a struggle, albeit a hopeless one for the victim, and unfortunately for the stoat, in a very exposed position in the middle of a field.

It was not long before this activity attracted the resident pair of crows who flew down to challenge the stoat for its meal, or just to make trouble. The crows bravely approached to within a couple of feet of the stoat and its dying quarry, one of the birds even trying to tweak the animal's black tipped tail.

Then just as it was getting interesting a buzzard came down to investigate, the crows flew off and by this time the stoat, not seeming to like all this attention, withdrew some distance away. The buzzard helped itself to what was now a corpse but it was getting towards dusk and it eventually flew away, to be replaced by a pair of magpies.

The stoat would be back later to finish the job.

A Page from the Diary

Lovely calm, warm day, long sunny periods. Two ravens and two Buzzards soaring overhead (am). The Ravens much higher than the Buzzards, spiralling up until they were literally specks in the blue sky. Identifiable largely by their croaking, although quite faint at that height. What an amazing sight! Still picking sweet peas, and apples from the orchard, to give away! Some butterflies still about. Heron flying down to water (pm). Fights of Greylag geese passing over. Grey Wagtail around water, front of mill (am). Later five Buzzards soaring high overhead. Some time after, two over yard garden 'mewing' to each other. Mallard pair on water behind mill. Little Owl calling at dusk.

A Page from the Diary

February 21st 2009

Bright spring morning. Song thrush singing, Mallard pair on the water, Kingfisher calling by water, Snowdrops now perfect and Aconites. Later beautiful sunny day, blue sky, quite warm. Goldfinches and Chaffinches around garden. Late morning… three Buzzards soaring high in the blue sky right over garden! Mewing calls drew my attention before they slanted off in a semi dive towards the nearby village. Tree Creeper in wood by the river, disturbed Barn Owl from barn early eve, Kestrel close to nest hole.

CHAPTER X

Shepherding

Starting my new life in an agricultural landscape it was never going to be long before I came into contact with livestock. Farming in this part of the Trent valley is largely arable, but forty years ago when I moved here there were many more animals around than there are now. There was still a dairy farm in the village at that time, now alas gone, and the buildings converted to new housing.

That was the last one, but when I was growing up in these parts every village had its dairy herds, and cows being walked down the road to and from the milking parlour were an everyday sight. Working horses were also a feature of the farming scene at that time as were pigs, poultry, beef cattle and in many cases, sheep.

Having cattle for neighbours when I first moved to the farm I quickly realised that something would have to be done about my boundary fences. On one side my land was adjacent to a very large field in which it was usual for a herd of bullocks to be kept, and on occasions even a bull. To complicate matters I was not aware then that it is an accepted responsibility for owners of animals to fence their stock in, rather than their neighbours having to fence them out.

The beasts were large, somewhat excitable and very intimidating at times, as well as being inclined to force their way through the rather poor combination of fence and hedge, which bounded my land. Well, when this occurred I could not just stand by and let it happen so Lydia and I, armed with sticks, had to try to drive them back to their own field. This was not easy as they did not want to go back, and as fast as we managed to persuade them to retreat through the gap they came through, they would run further up the hedge and enter by another weak spot.

This was farcical and even dangerous we thought, and as I had little confidence in the next door farmer properly addressing the matter, I arranged for the boundary to be re -fenced at my expense, so putting an end to the problem once and for all.

At about this time I agreed to let Arthur, the dairy farmer from the village graze some of his young heifers in a small field by the barns. All went well for a while, but one morning I got up to find the beasts all over my drive and roaming freely in the direction of my garden, which at that time they could have accessed.

I had to drive to Newark to catch a train for London early that day and had no time to round up cattle and mend fences, so I drove down to the village where I found Arthur in his milking parlour, busy with the morning routine with the cows.

I told him of the break out and hoped that he would go and recover the situation before too much damage was done. The incident did little for my peace of mind however, as I sped up to London on the train, picturing in my mind the animals all over my lawn by this time, so I decided there and then that I would have to tell him to find somewhere else for his extra grazing.

You learn by experience in these situations and having by this time considered sheep as an alternative and easier to control way of keeping the grass down, I embarked on a plan to securely fence all my land to stop livestock either getting in or getting out. This proved to be a costly project but for peace of mind it was worth every penny spent. Now I could keep animals without worrying about them when I was absent, or concern myself with invading cattle.

Thus started my adventure with sheep. I commenced by `borrowing` some from Bob, a friend who farmed in Warwickshire, but there soon proved to be a weakness in this arrangement in that being so far away I was reluctant to bother him when things went wrong, and attempted to deal with any problems myself.

This led to me getting the vet in to deal with foot rot, an expensive mistake which was not repeated. Accordingly when ever I saw a sheep limping, which often happened with those particular animals, I had to catch it and treat it using a recommended 'blue stick' which conveyed antiseptic to the offending area.

Well could I catch them? No, I discovered they can run fast and jump amazingly, even with an infected foot. I did not possess a shepherd's crook but my brother Nigel came to help me and we both rather made fools of ourselves making flying tackles in order to clutch their back legs and get them on their backs for treatment, in most cases only to finish up flat on our faces in the mud. This could not go on!

The sheep went back to where they came from, with my thanks. I had after all learned something from the experience but I then got in touch with another Bob, a local farmer who agreed to let me have sheep and lambs in the spring which I could keep until Autumn in order to keep the grass down.

Since then they have been delivered every year, made up partly of Jacobs with their characteristic 'patchwork' colouring and curly horns, and also some Scottish 'black face' ewes. Most of the ewes have very small lambs in tow when they arrive and are a constant source of interest and entertainment, not only to me, but also to any ramblers who pass by on the bridleway.

This arrangement has proved to be ideal and I still have sheep from him to this day. If they get foot troubles Bob deals with them, as he does with shearing, worming or anything else, but I am responsible for their day to day care which includes making sure they always have enough drinking water and moving them to fresh grazing whenever they get bored with their surroundings.

Things do however go wrong on occasions and one day a ewe fell, or was chased, in to the river. Tragically the animal must have become stuck in the mud, and having a thick fleece which would be heavy when saturated, could not climb out and was subsequently drowned.

Once or twice a ewe and sometimes a lamb has made it across the water and entered a wood on the other side from where it is impossible to get them out without help. The normal method is for Bob to come with Monica his wife and other members of his family to assist in rounding up the escapee, which is no easy feat when it runs backwards and forwards in panic through the dense undergrowth, and cannot even be seen half the time.

They never make the job easy by going back across the river to rejoin the flock, and the rest of their `family` show not the slightest interest.

One winter we put a batch of well grown lambs or hogs on some neighbouring land around a gravel pit. The area was fenced off, except along the water`s edge and for a few days all seemed well. Shortly before Christmas however and well after dark, I received a phone call from someone to tell me that his dog had got into the area via the water and chased two of the sheep into the lake.

It transpired that one sheep had drowned and the other had run off down the road to the village and taken refuge in my one-time solicitor's garage! This was embarrassing, they looked attractive grazing along the lake edges but the initiative had proved unsafe and had to be abandoned.

On the other side of the coin, the sheep have proved in spite of everything to be a great success. I look forward to their arrival with the new lambs in the spring, and they keep the grass in trim throughout the growing season. Although some of the fields are left to hay and wild flowers in the spring, the sheep clean them up afterwards ready for the winter. Come November I am always sorry to see them go.

Is there a lovelier or more pastoral scene than a flock of sheep wandering in and out of a ground hugging mist on a fine autumn day? Or gangs of little lambs racing around a field as the sun sets on a spring evening? At times like these any tasks associated with their care throughout the year seem of little account.

A Page from the Diary

April 8th 2012

A bright start to Easter day after rain in the night. Kingfisher perched

amongst cherry blossom over the water upstream.   Saw its reflection

first, bright blue in the water (from kitchen window)! What a lovely

sight to start the day. Mallard drake on water, Kestrel uttering its

excited 'courtship' calls near mill.   Later Kestrel flying around mill

and over barns.   Many Goldfinches in the trees.   Grey Wagtails

around yard garden.   A single Buzzard 'mewing' as it soared high

over the house (pm).   Pair of Green Woodpeckers in ha ha field,

Chiffchaffs singing from plantations.   Beautiful white Egret feeding in

water below bridge (pm). Jumped up and down and flapped its wings

repeatedly… seemed to assist in catching prey! Lambs fascinated by

hen Pheasant walking amongst them… very curious! Single Orange

Tip butterfly in garden.   Heron gliding low over 'new' orchard (pm).

Transplanted many primroses to new orchard, hope they will spread,

look lovely and mix well with the jonquils… same colour!

A Page from the Diary

Beautiful morning, misty at first, only a light breeze.   Six Whooper Swans flew over low from south east, calling to each other as they flew. First Blackcap singing, Woodpecker 'drumming', Goldfinches, Blackbirds, Chaffinches, Chiffchaff etc. also singing, along with very loud Wrens.   Sparrow Hawk 'dashed' past yard garden.   'Chorus' of Blackbird song mid afternoon, quite lovely....and Skylarks singing all day from beyond my southern boundary.   Green Woodpecker calling out, many Black Headed Gulls overhead feeding on flying insects I suspect, quite noisy.   Blackthorn in flower on the hedges. Butterflies on the wing, including Peacock and Tortoiseshell,   Song thrush and Robins singing loudly (pm) and much 'yaffling' from Green Woodpecker.   Buzzard glided low overhead.

CHAPTER XI

Evening Walks and Big Skies

I have always been fascinated by the period after sunset, the hours leading towards dusk, especially when the light lasts to ten or ten thirty pm and the temperature is mild. This is a special time, a wind down after the pace and activities of the day, when it is often possible to witness events in the natural world which either do not occur, or simply go under the radar in the middle of the day.

As the light fades and the sun sets, I love to walk out to see what is happening as most creatures prepare to sleep and others emerge to feed and hunt during the dark hours.

On a warm evening the first thing I notice are the scents from cut grass and blossoms, especially when the may is out and its perfume hangs in the air. The white flowers which decorate the hawthorn trees emit an instantly recognisable aroma which always seems at its strongest as the day begins to wane, and for me instantly sums up the very essence of the countryside.

Some say it is unlucky to bring these flowers in to the house which is a pity as they are so decorative and the scent amazing. But then I once knew a man who claimed that bringing any white flowers inside was tempting misfortune! All a question of what you believe I suppose?

The lambs in the field by the barns provide much entertainment, chasing around in gangs and jumping and leaping over each other, watched with only mild interest by the ewes. This behaviour appears to be almost entirely triggered by the setting sun and lasts for anything up to a couple of hours.

Rabbits appear from out of the undergrowth and if I keep still they often approach to within a yard or two, especially the baby ones.

The bird song gradually quietens down and it is interesting to note which birds sing the latest. There is usually a choir of blackbirds and song thrushes earlier on, together with some of the warblers and robins. Magpies `chatter` as they prepare to roost, the carrion crows sit quietly on the power lines, and a kestrel indulges in some last minute hunting before dark.

Sometimes a buzzard glides low over the field on its way to roost, the jackdaws are quiet and pairs of mallard fly around before pitching back down on to the water. Herons will often come down to feed in the river shallows looking almost prehistoric, their loud rasping calls and huge wings reminiscent of how we imagine pterodactyls, their dinosaur ancestors, to have looked in the darkening sky. Bats emerge and fly up and down the drive, often almost brushing my face as I stand and watch. A fox crosses the field.

The last singer is invariably a song thrush which on some nights is still pouring forth its song from a nearby tree top when it is virtually dark.

I look at the moon and the big sky and marvel at the clear expanse and the remains of receding clouds before I notice the north star, already burning bright in the gathering dusk. Sometimes I witness the moon rising above the distant hills. Crescent shaped as it emerges from the horizon and, when full, appearing huge, especially when shining through mist or surrounded by an orange glow as the clouds part.

But I wait for the barn owl and it is not too long before the ghostly white shape leaves the barn and flies low and silently over the sheep on its usual hunting beat, following the hedgerows and quartering the neighbouring fields. When they have young, and voles are plentiful, I notice that they return with prey about every fifteen minutes but in scarcer times the birds can be gone for a half hour or more.

Very much creatures of habit, each owl seems to follow its own individual route when hunting, night after night, although when out in the daytime they often seem to choose different directions, presumably according to availability of prey.

When bringing in food for the young they usually fly low as they near the barn, but sometimes the birds approach at a surprisingly high altitude and dive down with half closed wings to the entrance, almost falcon like. I never knew they did this.

Tawny owls are usually somewhere around and hoot intermittently from the wooded areas, and the mewing call of the little owl carries far across the fields. In late spring young tawny owls can be heard 'chirruping' from somewhere amongst the trees in the orchard or the plantations as it gets dark. These owls fledge much earlier than the barn owls, as the tawny lays eggs in February or March, and the somewhat monotonous calls of the young are a signal to the adults to come and feed them. Otherwise as the light finally fades, silence embraces the landscape.

True darkness is almost achievable here, light pollution is fairly minor and at night the stars can be spectacular. I just wish I knew the names of more of the planets. I recognise the North Star, Orion's Belt and the Plough but to my shame, little more. The milky way is clearly visible, especially on winter nights when the frost bites and the sky is really black, and I never cease to wonder at its vastness and the myriads of twinkling lights.

There is another world out there while we sleep and the distant bark of a fox and the occasional hoot or shriek from an owl reminds me that for some, this is their time, a thought which together with the sound of the rushing water, still fires my imagination and strangely comforts me through the night.

A Page from the Diary

March 31st 2013

Beautiful sunny clear morning. Pair of Bullfinches feeding on buds of trees behind coalhouse. Very smart Mallard drake on grass behind mill. Brilliant but cold day, wind stronger (pm) and from north east. Two Ravens flew fairly low over house and barns (pm), croaking loudly and 'rolling' in the wind. Amazing. Headed south east towards the Trent hills which still have patches of snow on them. Very few song birds about and little bird song for time of year. Chaffinches trying their best but the searching cold winds seem to be putting most birds off. Having said that Greenfinch sang briefly (pm)... not heard one for a while. Fieldfares still roosting in trees by first drive gate.

A Page from the Diary

Sunny, fresher start. Kingfisher fishing from back yard wall (am).

Eve, a Bat flew into the kitchen through open window, round and

round it went, almost brushing my face at times. Caught it with

child's fishing net! Later watched the owl family at dusk. At least

three young fledged and flying around the barns. Parents coming in

with prey. Quite magical. Also saw a bat flying along the drive.

Huge clamour from geese around lake areas, obviously started flocking

already. Must be hundreds judging by the noise.

CHAPTER XII

Owls

Halloween, October 31st and the dusk is early. Shrouds of mist encircle the farm buildings and there is a wintry nip in the air which suggests a frost as I talk to Michael, the gardener, about jobs completed and those which need to be done before winter proper sets in.

A white shape approaches out of the mist, then veers away to the entrance to the building where the barn owls are raising a very late second brood. The owl is carrying prey, a vole or a mouse, and on arrival at the nest there is an excited hissing and 'snoring' from the almost fully fledged owlets, which have been waiting at the entrance for yet another meal.

The owl soon floats off in to the mist with a 'strangled' screech, which sounds even more eerie than usual as it resumes its almost constant hunting in order to satisfy the ever hungry and now full size fledglings. Within minutes the other parent arrives, also carrying prey, and once again there is a frenzy of screeching and hissing from the young as they greedily seize the vole, which is swallowed whole by whichever is the most dominant or more hungry of the owlets.

The mysterious white owls flying in and out of the gathering mist and the screeching and hissing of the young are enough to frighten anyone unfamiliar with their ways, should they be passing close by in the gloaming on this Halloween eve. We were standing within a few yards of the nest site and the owls showed little fear, but the noise from the barn was potentially startling and would sound very strange to anyone unused to the ways of these birds. Little wonder the barn owl used to be surrounded by superstition and even fear in days gone by.

Who needs ghosts or ghouls, 'trick or treating' or candles in hollowed out pumpkins on a night like this?

The year must be a very good one for voles, the owls' principal prey. A second brood is unusual for barn owls and only occurs when there is a surfeit of food i.e. the vole population is unusually high. Young owls fledging in November will not have a great chance of survival if the winter proves very wet or cold, but we wish them well.

I confess to having been fascinated by this bird ever since I found a nest with five almost round white eggs in a hollow tree when I was about twelve years old. I later went back to see the young owls and I remember clearly the sight of their slightly comical faces and black eyes as I peered into the cavity from the top of a ladder. I remember too the weird shrieks from the adults when I disturbed them from their tree and they floated off into the dusk.

Of course it is now illegal to disturb a barn owl at its nest without a license, as these birds are not as numerous as they once were. Their numbers 'crashed' in the 1960s and 70s and they became comparatively rare in many parts of the country where they were once a familiar sight.

This reduction in their numbers can in part be attributed to the loss of suitable nest sites resulting from Dutch elm disease and the conversion and replacement of old barns and other buildings which they formerly occupied. Changes in farming practices have with little doubt also been a factor but there has been something of a recovery in recent years, due to an increasingly widespread provision of nest boxes.

The barn owl, unlike its familiar relative the tawny or wood owl, does not frequent built up areas and so is not normally seen in or around towns or cities, even in leafy suburban districts. It is a bird of open countryside where it hunts the fields, hedges and dykes and also, like the kestrel, the wide verges of country roads.

Living for some time within a semi urban district, my encounters with this bird in recent times had been few and far between, but on buying the farm and putting myself back in to a country setting I hoped to renew my acquaintance with the ghostly hunter?

I had to wait some time. Having old barns, to say nothing of the mill, and being in such a quiet location amidst suitable territory I was optimistic, but for years I only very occasionally caught sight of one, usually from the car whilst driving at night. The buildings seemed ideal and I could hardly believe the absence of even former use by owls, like old food pellets on the floors or the odd feather.

I asked Keith the joiner who regularly does work around the house and buildings and has long ago ceased to be fazed by anything unusual I ask him to do, if he would make me a nest box. In the event an old wooden apple box which we found in one of the barns was modified to suit and duly erected high up in a small barn which I then locked up to minimise disturbance. We then had to make an entrance to the building in the gable end to provide access for the owls.

For three or four years nothing happened. I went in to the barn to check now and again to look for pellets but there was no sign of any owl activity. Then, one winter day I saw an owl flying along a ditch, just a few hundred yards from the barn and I just wondered, could this be what I had been waiting for? A few days later I saw the bird again and this time it flew straight to the barn containing the nest box.

This was a magic moment! I could hardly believe my luck. The thought that there may be a pair and that they might decide to make their home in my barn, just a short distance from the house, was exciting. From then on I kept a lookout when ever I had the opportunity, and sure enough it wasn't long before I observed two owls leaving the barn to hunt. I knew then that my efforts had been rewarded and it would only be a matter of time before nesting might take place.

I was overjoyed, what a privilege in this day and age to have wild breeding barn owls living within a few yards of my house. My thoughts went back to that day, all those years ago when I found the nest in a hollow tree. I was going to relive that experience and much, much more!

From then on things never looked back. The owls have so far nested every season for seventeen years and have only once failed to raise a brood. I regularly watch the adults out hunting on summer evenings, and also often in the early mornings. They seem to show little fear of me and regularly fly within a few yards of where I am standing.

On one occasion one of the birds flew straight towards me, as though to perch on my head, and only swerved away at the last second. Maybe it mistook me for a post?

I have even watched barn owls hunting from the comfort of a settee in my drawing room. Floating, hovering, twisting and turning over the long grass and the buttercups on a June evening, sometimes backlit by the setting sun, there are few sights more rewarding or more reminiscent of the countryside of long ago.

Hearing them screech at night is always a thrill and once one of the young owls perched on my bedroom window sill and looked in on me. How amazing was that? I even hear their strange calls close by, when sitting in the kitchen as the owls fly around the mill after dark.

The young in most years emerge from the barn in June or July and sit around on the buildings waiting for their parents to bring prey. At these times the adults can frequently be seen hunting in bright sunshine, even in the middle of the day, but interestingly they do not seem to be seriously mobbed by crows, as is often the case with other birds of prey.

In some years a pair of kestrels nest in another box only yards from the barn owl's site and in the same building. When the owls are out in the daytime some conflict can occur, for both birds hunt very similar prey and an element of competition is perhaps not surprising. If the owls waited until dark before emerging confrontations would be avoided, but in spite of their daylight excursions I have only once seen a serious challenge by the more agile kestrels.

I came out of the house early one evening in summer and was going about my business when my attention was drawn to shrill screeching noises from up in the sky. I looked up and was amazed to see a barn owl and a kestrel seemingly locked together by their talons like a large feathery ball in mid air. The birds fell downwards, the owl on top and the kestrel underneath, still locked together, and crashed into a small tree where they stayed for a few seconds before both flew out apparently unharmed and went off in different directions.

Another remarkable and unexpected close encounter which I could never have imagined. Yet I learn not to be too surprised by anything I am fortune enough to witness here.

A Page from the Diary

Dark morning, continuous and at times heavy rain. Cold. Stoat on front lawn, rolling over and over and performing acrobatics... to entice prey? Then proceeded to river bank behind back yard to hunt. Disturbed Barn Owl from nesting barn (am). Orange Tip butterflies on the wing. Five eggs in Jackdaw's nest in box in big barn. Oyster Catcher flying over. Beautiful warm, sunny afternoon. Water Vole near its hole in river bank behind mill. Appeared to be eating grass, then dived into water and immediately submerged. Perfect rainbow, evening as the sun was going down. Garden Warbler singing and Lesser Whitethroat. River in 'spate' (pm).

A Page from the Diary

November 27th and 28th 2010

First snow of the winter, approx. ½", looks very crisp and cold.   Very frosty in night, large moon and starry sky early am, very beautiful. Blackbirds busy eating berries around garden.   Song thrush 'subsong' again.   Many Pochard on lake including pair of Crested Pochard, also gulls and Coots.   Two pairs of Mallard on water behind mill with Moorhens.   Some Fieldfares about, small groups.

Beautiful crisp, very cold morning, snow covering everything still unmelted, blue sky, no wind!   What could be better?   Ice on river by ford, Fieldfares, Mistle thrush, Blackbirds and Robins in orchard eating apples.   Squirrel running about.   Redwing upstream.   Four pairs of Mallard on water upstream.   Nb   Ice on inside of bedroom window this morning!   Brilliant moon last night.

112

CHAPTER XIII

A Winter Afternoon

It is December and the days around the time of the winter solstice are dark and short. The human population are busy Christmas shopping and the countryside around here is quiet, except for orange clad engineers working on the nearby railway line.

They have been there all weekend laying new track, and in the gathering dusk I can see a long row of twinkling lights glinting through the trees, like a Christmas decoration or a string of harbour lights. The lights enable work to be carried out right through the night and I being very probably the only witness to what is going on, the comparative remoteness of my situation seems strangely heightened by this activity.

The road from the village and the level crossing on the railway are closed and the distant rail laying and aligning work provide the only sounds other than those of the natural world.

The wild creatures know nothing of Christmas shopping or railway operations and shut away here in the last hours before dark there is spread out beneath the orchard trees a veritable feast for all to enjoy. Redwings and fieldfares, those much travelled thrushes which come here to escape the frozen winters of their northern homelands, flit about nervously between the trees and the banquet of fallen apples which lie in the dew soaked grass.

They are right to be wary for the local sparrow hawk is likely to view this as a feast of a different kind and will dash in without warning, often only inches above the ground. Any unsuspecting thrush will provide a vital supper for the hawk as the long winter night approaches.

Success is never guaranteed however, and the thrushes will scatter in all directions before cautiously resuming their own vital meal of rotting windblown apples. Pheasants, magpies, jackdaws, blackbirds, robins and blue and great tits are also in the orchard to take advantage of the natural bounty, and even the carrion crow will visit, though being more wary than his fellow diners, will stay in a tree, keeping an eye on proceedings, before hastily snatching an apple and flying a little way off to eat it in the open field.

Rats and squirrels will not be far away and even moorhens will take advantage of the free harvest when the weather is cold.

Earlier in the afternoon the geese came over. Like advancing aircraft, their voices audible well before they came in to sight, wave after wave of local greylags flying low overhead in V formation heading for their roosting lakes and darkening the sky as they passed. There must have been several hundred and although I witness similar sights almost on a daily basis at this time of year, I cannot help but stand and stare, and listen to the music of their cries as they swiftly fade away in the darkening skies.

A buzzard flies low over a plantation and will soon go to roost and the sound of jays in the woodland floats across on the clammy air, their raucous cries sounding like a quarrel, but they are probably protesting at the early emergence of a tawny owl after its daytime sleep.

Later as darkness finally takes over I hear close by the quavering hoot of the owl carrying far into the still night. I put another log on the fire and watch the flames eagerly licking the chimney piece. There will be a frost tonight but the feast is over for the day and the fieldfares and redwings will be roosting in the tall thorn hedges where they should be safe for the night. They will be back in the orchard at first light to feed again, especially if the ground is frozen making insects hard to find.

It will soon be Christmas and even colder conditions and possibly snow may well be on the way, making life hard for all wild things but if so the 'apple feast' may prove a life saver for some.

A Page from the Diary

Dull start, cooler (very welcome). Male Sparrow Hawk flying over house carrying prey. Kingfisher fishing behind house. Grey Wagtails and Robins busy feeding nestlings (pm). Kingfisher fishing from wire under bridge. Goldfinches, Greenfinches and Bullfinches about. Sand Martins in the sky! Oyster Catcher flying low over garden, Swifts flying. Green Woodpecker drinking from water behind mill. All in one view, Green Woodpecker, two Moorhens, Grey Wagtail and two Rabbits! Lots of butterflies incl. Red Admiral, Tortoiseshell, Small Copper, Brimstone, Meadow Browns etc. Also gorgeous blue Damsel flies. Kingfisher fishing from sheep hurdle behind mill (eve). 20 Lapwings flew low over house (eve)... silent! Later 11 Lapwings flew in opposite direction.

A Page from the Diary

June 12th 2017

Overcast, breezy, warm.

Three pairs of Tufted duck on water and a Heron wading at the edge (am).

Kingfisher around bridge and Egret wading just beyond… watched while having my supper.

Jackdaws continually 'dive bombing' Carrion Crow in ash tree behind house. A few minutes later immature Heron came down and started fishing, then followed by a Mallard duck and her brood of ducklings. All watched within a half hour while sitting at the kitchen table.

At the same time Tufted duck pair diving in water behind house, plus a Moorhen.

Same eve at dusk, Heron came down to fish three or four yards from window, almost darkening the sky with its huge wings as it passed the window. Young Tawny Owls 'chirruping' near orchard, faint 'snoring' coming from Barn Owl nest

CHAPTER XIV

Reflections

This morning I awoke to an orange coloured sky. The bedroom was filled with the glow from the rising sun and when I looked out of the window a skein of greylag geese flew past the house, their voices enlivening the stillness of the dawn and the birds backlit by the orange light. What a spectacular start to the day, like a Peter Scott painting. Everyone should wake to an orange coloured sky!

Looking back on this moment led me to think about the many wonderful scenarios which I have been privileged to witness during my time here. It has truly been a life changing journey, bringing unexpected rewards at every level. The sights and sounds of the countryside and close encounters with the local wild life which I enjoy on a daily basis have been beyond all expectations.

My often unique adventures and the things I have experienced since moving into this waterside country location have been consistently more interesting and in some ways stranger, than anything I could have envisaged. And they continue to be so.

It has not however all been 'sweetness and light'. There have been dark days, and one of the darkest was the experience of an attempted break in during the night. Not too long after I had moved in I was awakened at around midnight by the sound of voices; not a good thing to happen in my situation, being alone in the house and remote from any lawful human activity. Almost immediately there was the sound of breaking glass and some loud noises from the rear of the house.

I got out of bed and the only thing I could think of to do was go downstairs and switch the outside lights on. This I did, together with a number of lights in the house and to my huge relief the next thing I heard was the sound of the intruders running away down the garden path. They were in a hurry to leave as they even broke the garden gate by trying to leap over it!

It would seem that they did not realise that anyone was living here, probably due to the fact that builders' materials and equipment were outside, some of the alteration work being currently underway, and there were no lights showing at the time.

They had broken one of the kitchen windows and got inside through a temporarily boarded up rear doorway but could not get to the rest of the house, or to me, due to some secure bolts which were fitted to two internal doors.

It was all quite a shock and for some years afterwards I never felt the same about retiring for the night. To this day I find myself listening for any unusual sounds should I be lying awake.

I was very lucky only to suffer minor damage and a bit of a fright. Was someone or something watching over me once again?

A few days after the attempted break in a police constable came round to offer me counselling, but by then my independent spirit had largely returned, at least in daylight hours, and I politely declined!

My water supply is laid under a neighbouring field, and one year the ground was deep ploughed without any regard for the pipe which was broken in several places. The pipe had been there for a great many years, indeed well before I bought the property, and it was known to the farmer, but presumably this time the contractors never got the message.

Subsequently Kieron the plumber re-sited the supply around the edge of the field, hopefully out of harms way, but this was a lengthy and costly operation involving the hire of a digger for several days. It was inconvenient being without water for the best part of a week, but the incident did serve as a reminder of our good fortune in having running water 'on tap'. Maybe I should have kept the well after all!

It was suggested to me before I first saw the place that there used to be otters here many years ago, a comment that helped to arouse my interest in the property. For a long time I clung to the thought that maybe, just maybe, I might be lucky enough to see one if I lived here long enough.

They say 'everything comes to those who wait' and amazingly one morning when looking upstream from the bathroom window I spotted a head, not a duck, making a bow wave in the water close to the bypass sluice. The head emerged from the water, followed by a long body and long tail and climbed up onto the bank in my full view. It was an otter.

I could hardly believe what I was seeing. I have watched otters on occasion on the west coast of Scotland where they are now quite numerous, but to see one from my own bathroom window was more than I could have hoped for. It stood in full sunlight for about a minute, its thick fur glistening with water droplets, then slipped down in to the overflow stream and out of sight.

Once or twice I suspected that I might have heard one 'whistling' at night and sombody passing on the bridleway once told me he had seen one, but this was my first and so far only confirmation. I have found opened, but not broken, fresh water mussel shells on the river banks though and wondered if this could be the work of otters?

The otter sighting made for a real 'red letter day,' but then I never expected to be able to watch snowy white egrets feeding within yards of my window almost on a daily basis whilst having my breakfast, or nesting grey wagtails in the back yard. I never really thought that kingfishers would be racing up and down stream or that stoats would be performing acrobatics on the lawn.

It is thought that these antics by the stoat are a hunting ploy designed to entice or even hypnotise small birds in to a false sense of security. I have not so far witnessed such an outcome from these games but can well believe the theory to be true.

I have mentioned in an earlier chapter, the stoat's apparent disregard of my presence when hunting and I still find it interesting that these animals will at times hunt and even kill within a few yards of where I am standing, presumably blood lust or hunger overcoming any fear. Even weasels can be remarkably bold but a fox or badger will always run away when disturbed.

One hot summer morning I came across a weasel sleeping in the sunshine at the edge of the lawn. I stood within three or four feet of it, keeping perfectly still and although it stirred and disappeared under some nearby tall plants it soon emerged again and continued to doze, curled up in a circle, and seemingly unaware (or unconcerned) by my closeness.

Whilst on the subject of stoats and weasels and their kin, I discovered one evening, and much to my surprise, a family of polecats. They emerged from the undergrowth by a hedge, again within no more than a few feet of where I was standing. There seemed to be several young ones, or 'kits' which kept popping in and out of the vegetation and staring at me without showing any fear.

With pretty faces and yellowish ears, black legs and a quite bushy black tail they were of striking appearance and a most unexpected sight. I had no idea that these chiefly nocturnal hunters lived so close to me. I had never seen one before, but thinking about it, they may well have bred in a large log pile at the bottom of the orchard which is completely undisturbed and situated at the meeting point of the main waterway and the overflow stream.

Polecats have increased in recent years and spread from their former Welsh stronghold into much of lowland England, but as usual I never know what to expect here and it seems at times as though almost anything is possible!

Rooks interest me, albeit in a very different way. Although closely related to the carrion crow and of similar size, unlike that bird you do not often see them in towns and cities. They are associated perhaps more than any other with farmland and their presence, their sociable habits and their raucous, although sometimes quite musical calls seem the very essence of the countryside.

Every afternoon or early evening, particularly in late summer or autumn I notice a constant stream of these birds, one to two hundred strong, often accompanied by jackdaws, passing overhead at high altitude on their way to their traditional roosting site which appears to be in the wooded escarpments on the far side of the river Trent.

They come from the direction of their nesting trees a mile or so upstream and always follow the same course, pretty much directly over my house, sometimes playing games in the air with jackdaws as they go on their way. I like to think that they are using a traditional and old established flight path, perhaps followed by generations of rooks.

I was delighted when a family of little fox cubs appeared in the garden and I watched them playing in the dusk from my windows. But something mysterious happened when I visited a fox earth upstream one night and five small cubs came out to play within three or four yards of me. This was I thought remarkable, they showed no fear, just mild curiosity as they stared at me wide eyed. This was the kind of thing I used to dream of when I was a child, but never thought I would experience. It was the stuff of nature books, pictures and stories about the wild which I treasured and read avidly when growing up.

The experience was so rewarding that I went up the field again at the same time the following night, hoping for a repeat performance, but no cubs appeared. Feeling disappointed and a little puzzled I walked around a little further from the earth only to find a fox cub lying dead in the grass, seemingly unmarked and showing no sign of any molestation. On searching further I eventually found all five cubs, all dead and all unmarked.

This was an immensely sad outcome, after such a close and quite touching encounter only the previous night. The idyllic scene which I discovered had only lasted a day! It was hard to take in what had happened, but the episode showed just how fragile and unpredictable life in the wild can be. The only answer I could think of was that they may all have eaten some poisoned bait from somewhere, but I could not be sure.

I was in the right place at the right time one day, when I found a baby barn owl in the yard garden, shivering and alone, looking more like a ball of discarded sheep's wool than a bird. It had evidently fallen from the nest in the barn and crawled through a hole at the bottom of the door. I was able to pick it up and return it to the nest from where it later fledged along with its siblings but this was a close call as it could not fly and would never have made it back without my help.

My timing was right again when one night I followed two badgers, beautifully illuminated by my car headlights, as they trotted side by side all the way up the drive until they turned through the hedge in to the orchard.

There is evidence of badger activity all around and there is at least one sett upstream in the river banks, but in view of their nocturnal habits I do not often see them. I do however see the results of their diggings, including evidence of freshly dug out wasp nests in the summer.

It is interesting on wet nights to find on occasions the drive to be covered in frogs, and I mean hundreds of them. They are presumably attracted by the adjacent gravel pit lake, but they do not move and it is almost impossible to avoid running over them. Why so many of them just sit on what is now a tarmac drive, not apparently having any inclination to find somewhere safer I do not know. The phenomenon only occurs maybe one night in the year, and I think has something to do with their mating behaviour, but there may be other reasons?

Nesting tawny and little owls, kestrels and green woodpeckers I have never taken for granted, nor the regular appearance of sparrow hawks and sometimes a hobby, that swift flying little falcon which hunts down swallows, martins, dragonflies and other flying insects.

I love the family parties of long tailed tits, and I see goldcrests and sometimes the tree creeper but there has been a downside. Gone are the tree and house sparrows, nesting starlings and swallows, the cuckoo, turtle dove, spotted flycatchers, and snipe.

Even the yellow hammer which used to sing its song 'a little bit of bread and no cheese' which I learnt to recognise as a child is now comparatively scarce. They used to inhabit the hedgerows and seemed to sing all day long. I would see them coming down to the water to drink on hot days.

The corn bunting has disappeared and I miss its song which my father likened to 'jangling keys'. Yellow wagtails were a regular sight in the early days, running about on my lawn in the spring and summer months and in winter golden plover would feed in the surrounding fields, but I have not seen them for a few years. Lapwings are now scarce and yet were always regarded as very much a farmland bird in the past. Water voles are now rarely seen, but in my early years here they were resident in some numbers.

Some of these declines are localised and sometimes connected with food supply. There were sparrows, starlings and nesting swallows when I first moved in, but there had been cattle around the barns and in neighbouring fields at that time, whereas now there are only sheep. The spilt grain and foodstuffs for the pigs and poultry also probably made a difference. There are still house sparrows to be seen in the village just about a mile away. Maybe there is more food for them there?

Other species which have been lost however are part of a national and even international reduction in numbers due to changes in farming practices, possibly climate change and dangers which occur during migration.

But on the plus side, buzzards now soar overhead on fine days, their 'mewing' cries ringing through the air, and that is something I never expected to see. I am fairly sure one of them even roosts a little way upstream in one of the riverside ash trees, that is if they can escape detection by the carrion crows which give them little peace.

Egrets and oyster catchers are now regularly seen, and many more wild ducks and geese since the creation of the nearby gravel pit lakes. I still have pheasants, grey and red legged or 'French' partridges and finches, although linnets and greenfinches are not so common around the garden these days.

I still awake and sometimes go to bed listening to the song thrush, my favourite songster, and on spring days I hear the skylark`s song drifting on the breeze, so I mustn't grumble. I am a fortunate man.

How did I get here, I sometimes ask myself? I am living in a mini wild life paradise within half a mile of where I was born. I look at the foot bridge from my window every day, where my mother used to bring me as a baby in a pram to meet my father. He would be walking home from the Home Guard, where he served in the river patrol during the war years. But none of this was planned or ever envisaged, how could it be? It is all just a coincidence… or is it?

I now even see from time to time my father`s favourite bird, the raven, the largest member of the crow family and formerly only encountered in wild moorland or mountain areas and around sea cliffs.

This is perhaps the biggest surprise of all. I have watched them so many times, in the West country, Wales, Cumbria and in Scotland, but never thought to see one here. My father would not have thought it possible back in the day, and whenever I hear that distinctive deep croak, unlike any other bird, and see these impressive birds passing swiftly overhead or soaring high in the sky I think of him.

He also loved to see wild geese and I think of him too when I hear their far off cries on a winter morning. High in the sky they come, in V formation, often a hundred or hundred and fifty strong, their high pitched calls sounding reminiscent of a pack of hunting dogs.

Always audible before I see them, strangely the sound when first heard does not always register. I accept the calls without immediately realising what is making them. Then I look up and see the ragged skein, always high and seemingly in a world of their own as they forge through the sky, the sunlight glinting on their wings. Usually too high to identify for sure but I think the geese which pass over here are, more often than not, whitefronts or pinkfeet.

One cold November morning I witnessed the passage of a large number of local greylags, probably running into hundreds, flying so low you could hear their wingbeats. This was good enough, but later the same morning a skein of wild whitefronts passed over, flying high and fast, their voices advertising their presence as they headed south for the winter. This was outstanding, and all in one day!

An extra treat occurred whilst working outside on a cold and very misty day. The mist was thick, indeed a fog, and the aspect decidedly wintry, when I became aware of a different, rather musical sound. The calls of whooper swans! The birds were almost hidden in the mist, their white shapes ghost like as they passed over, but there was no mistaking those calls. Like the wild geese these swans are migrants from northern lands and spend the winter months with us but I do not often see them.

I never know for sure what to expect from day to day but I am rarely short of surprises. Just when I think I have seen it all, I witness something completely unexpected which just stops me in my tracks and makes me count my good fortune.

I was out walking with the family in the 'ha ha' field one lazy summer afternoon when to my astonishment a red kite, the first and only one I have seen here, flew overhead and proceeded to circle quite low directly over the house for several minutes. Another magic moment, completely unexpected, almost as though 'staged' just for our delight.

Every day I see the river rushing by, I walk through flower meadows and listen to the birds in the spring and early summer, and I still look for the first snowdrops. I enjoy the frost covered landscape and the anticipation of hearing wild geese heading for some far away estuary or salt marsh. I am content in the early phase of autumn when the apples and plums festoon the trees and the smell of bonfire smoke lingers in the air. I am fascinated by the white mist which creeps over the landscape on autumn or winter evenings and I will never forget my first experience of a snowfall.

Everything as far as the eye could see was white, the fields, the trees, the buildings, the only exception being the water. I could not imagine a more spectacular scene and the endless snow, the dazzling effect of the sun, the blue sky and that fascinating silence which is so characteristic of snowfall made me feel like a child again.

On looking back, and attempting to evaluate all that I have been so fortunate to witness, it should be emphasised that this is not an area normally associated with spectacular wildlife. It is not the Somerset levels or the Norfolk coast, nor does it compare in any way with Wales, Cumbria or even the Derbyshire dales. This is simply a quiet corner of the east midlands, in a district dominated by agriculture.

My observations therefore cannot be in any way unique. It is just that I have been fortunate enough to live for a time where the natural world has come to me, rather than I having to go out and look for it.

These writings and the contents of my diary prove that nature is out there and all around us. For anyone interested enough to look, and to explore the countryside, there are rich rewards in store, no matter how familiar and 'ordinary' the landscape.

Life at the farm has been good. Any problems or disappointments are long behind me, and living so close to nature in all its moods has been a constant source of interest, and a joy beyond anything I could have envisaged.

Could it have been part of some grand plan? I shall never know. Such things are, perhaps rightly, beyond our understanding.

In the long scheme of things, I suppose it's all water under the bridge.